"IMMEDIATE RESPONSE
IS THE MOOD OF THE KINGDOM."
—John Shea, *Stories of God*

"THE SAVIOR SAVES WITH QUESTIONS,
YES AND FOREVER!"
—Mother Mary Francis, P.C.C., *Canto*

Gloria Hutchinson

JESUS' SAVING QUESTIONS

Nihil Obstat: Rev. Hilarion Kistner, O.F.M.
Rev. John J. Jennings

Imprimi Potest: Rev. Jeremy Harrington, O.F.M.
Provincial

Imprimatur: Rev. John L. Cavanaugh, V.G.
Archdiocese of Cincinnati
October 18, 1983

Cover and book design by Julie Lonneman.

SBN 0-86716-028-4

For those who
love the Word
and accept the challenge

CONTENTS

INTRODUCTION

If there was one thing that was clear about the Son of Man—even to those who saw him as just another zealous crackpot—it was his sense of urgency. He had a sacramental awareness of time, time as gift, time as treasure to be invested rather than buried in a field where procrastination would rot it away. Our ubiquitous plaques advising, "Always put off until tomorrow what you can do today," would be swept off the wall by the intense young rabbi who turned himself inside out trying to convince people to "get with it. You never know when your life may be demanded of you."

They called him "Teacher." And so he was. His stories deceptively simple in their everyday apparel, turned out to be hard nuts to crack. Two thousand years later we are still peeling away the shells to get at the sweet meat within such homely tales as "The Good Samaritan" and "The Buried Talents."

But the stories were only the beginning. He also had a way of asking questions that could nail a person to the wall or catapult his listener into expanded consciousness. Jesus of Nazareth didn't have time for idle questions that simply pass the time of day or fill the awkward silences. He was a tough-minded teacher intent on educating—leading out, moving on, prompting conversion.

If people stayed put after hearing his parables and absorbing his questions, Jesus had failed. Teaching for him was a matter of life or death. If people didn't get the point, if he couldn't get it through their thick hearts that the Kingdom was at hand (Hold your hand in front of your face and *see* how close it is!), they might as well be dead. And he might as well have spared himself the trouble of the Incarnation.

Although most of us have at least a passing acquaintance with the Gospel stories, we don't exactly go to the head of the class when it comes to interpreting Jesus' questions. We recall how he often used a query to elude the spring of a carefully constructed trap: "Show me a coin. Whose head is this? Whose

1

inscription do you read?" (Luke 20:24). Or we hear him seeking our attention, asking the puzzler he is eager to answer *for* us: "To what shall I compare the reign of God? It is like yeast..." (Luke 13:20-21).

But there are plenty more questions—about 140 recorded in the four Gospels—and most don't let the listener off the hook that easily. Could we walk away, unruffled and unaroused by the following:

> "Can you drink the cup I shall drink or be baptized in the same bath of pain as I?" (Mark 10:38)

> "If I am telling the truth,
> why do you not believe me?" (John 8:46)

> "And if you greet your brothers only, what is so praiseworthy about that? Do not pagans do as much?" (Matthew 5:47)

> "Tell me, why do you not judge for yourselves what is just?"
> (Luke 12:57)

All these questions are calculated to stop us in our tracks, force us into honest self-evaluation, fracture our complacency, keep us awake at night. We ignore them at our peril. They are the fisherman's bait—and if we don't bite, we risk the possibility that he may sail away without us.

Each of the following 10 chapters considers one of Jesus' questions. Each question is intended to define or divide; none may safely be answered by those who want to run in place.

Each question is first traced through the four Gospels and placed in the context of the event or events with which the evangelists have surrounded it.

Then the reader is invited to take the question personally, using the method of meditation St. Ignatius of Loyola taught in his *Spiritual Exercises*. Ignation meditation places a person inside a Gospel scene, aware of the sights, sounds and sensations of the moment, rubbing elbows with the people who witness the event.

In these pages the reader becomes a member of the Twelve.

As Jesus' question still hangs in the air, the reader is then invited to slip away from the crowd for a few moments and consider all the implications of the question before returning to give Jesus the answer for which he is waiting.

A prayer closes each chapter. The last chapter leads into night prayer with Jesus and the disciples, a service which might be celebrated with people from a prayer or study group who have also heard and pondered the Lord's questions.

When Jesus asks, "Who do you say that I am?" (Mark 8:29), the question is directed not only to Peter, James and John, but to *you*, the contemporary disciple, the person who has decided to sit still and listen, to allow Jesus to have his way with you by hearing and responding in a serious manner to his questions. There is no surer way into the heart of a great teacher.

One suggestion: Approach these questions with a clean slate. Heard as though for the first time, they can set off firecrackers and topple ancient temples. As Anselm Hunt observes in *Before the Deluge*, "Christ, like someone we desperately love, should be a perpetual surprise, a continuous fresh start." He is himself the most crucial question we will ever face.

CHAPTER ONE

WHO DO YOU SAY I AM?

> Then Jesus and his disciples set out for the villages
> around Caesarea Philippi. On the way he asked his
> disciples this question: "Who do people say that I am?"
> They replied, "Some, John the Baptizer, others, Elijah,
> still others, one of the prophets." "And you," he went on
> to ask, "who do you say that I am?" Peter answered him,
> "You are the Messiah!" Then he gave them strict orders
> not to tell anyone about him. (Mark 8:27-30)

UNLIKE THE WICKED QUEEN who envied Snow White,
most of us have learned that we can't trust our mirrors. When we
really want to know what kind of image we're projecting, we look
into the eyes of a friend and ask, "Whom do you see?" The
question betrays all the vulnerability of, "Do you love me?"
Hearing it from the mouth of Christ, we recognize how
completely he shared our need for affirmation.

We hunger for the validation of being known.

> "Yahweh, you examine me and you know me,..."
> (Psalm 139:1, *Jerusalem Bible*)

Identity is our dearest possession. We are unnerved by those who
expect us to be someone we are not, miscasting us in their
personal dramas when we haven't approved of the script. We
require the certainty that at least one other person knows who we
are and what we are about. When St. Francis prayed for the

grace to be understanding rather than to be understood, he already had the comfort of Sister Clare and Brother Leo who could read him like a familiar book.

Before their visit to Caesarea Philippi, Jesus and his disciples had been together for about a year. He had put them through an intensive basic training that toppled many of their cherished beliefs and favorite assumptions: When they ate, they were to set a place for the tax collector or the prostitute. If they were hungry on the sabbath, they should pick corn and share it; the sabbath was made not for their enslavement but for their enjoyment. They were to recognize as closest kin those who dedicated themselves to doing the Father's will. And when they hit the road, they were to do so with only their everyday tunics and their Master's potent message of repentance and forgiveness.

By the time they approached Caesarea Philippi, along the east bank of the Jordan in the territory of Philip the Tetrarch, the disciples had already moved far beyond the boundaries of their traditional beliefs. They had seen Jesus heal the incurably ill and heard him grant forgiveness to public sinners. They were astounded when he transformed a crazed and howling demoniac into a serenely rational recruit who then witnessed to God's mercy throughout the Decapolis, the 10 cities of Galilee.

Fresh in their minds was the power of his compassion, which enabled him to feed 4,000 people with a ration of bread and fish fit for a few dozen. They had reveled in the largeness of his spirit as they collected enough leftovers to last them for weeks. Among themselves they speculated over his identity. Was he Moses reincarnate, come back to triumph over Rome as he had over Egypt? Was he a prophet in whose shadow all others became minor figures in the story of salvation? Was he, by God, the promised Messiah himself?

They hadn't yet asked him. That took more nerve than they could muster. Just a few days earlier he had upbraided them for their miserable failure to perceive the significance of the multiplication of the loaves. He had been shocked at their thick-headedness, bombarding them with incredulous questions about sightless eyes and stopped-up ears. They weren't eager to wind up looking like dolts again so soon. The disciples kept their own counsel, hoping Jesus would give them the answer on a platter, without benefit of parables.

What he had revealed to the Samaritan woman (see John 4:25-26), Jesus had not, at this point, explicitly told his closest companions. Like a parent who elicits an important truth from a child, Jesus wanted the disciples to arrive at their own answer. Their joy, and his, would be greater if they drew wisdom up from their communal well.

In his spare style, Mark encapsulates the incident for us. His pen and ink sketch offers no emotional colors or scenic backdrops. Jesus asks two questions which appear, at first glance, almost identical. The disciples respond to the initial query, "Who do people say that I am?" (Mark 8:27), by dutifully reporting the gossip they've picked up on the waterfront, in the synagogue courtyards and among the crowds at the marketplace. They are passing on the common knowledge, neither disparaging nor subscribing to it. Peter alone responds to the second question, "And you,…who do you say that I am?" (Mark 8:29), with a knowledge so rare and certain that it could only come from above. The responses are as far apart as news bulletins and lyric poetry.

"Who do you say that I am?" is a turning point in Mark's Gospel. Once his friends have recognized him at Caesarea Philippi, Jesus can set his face toward Jerusalem. He is free to open up the mystery of the Messiah, carefully but firmly paring away the encrusted expectations of military glory and merciless vengeance on the enemies of the Chosen People. He is free to divulge that the Messiah is armed only with compassion and forgiveness, that the Messiah and Isaiah's suffering servant are one.

From this point on, whenever the disciples try to impose a man-made Messianic identity on him, Jesus will rebuke them. They must learn that the way to the Kingdom is paved with peace and attained through mercy. Jesus' entire ministry depends on an understanding of this truth.

While Mark tells us little about the Son of Man's reaction to Peter's revelation, Matthew (16:17-20) elaborates. "Simon, son of Jonah, you are a happy man!" Jesus exclaims. "Because it was not flesh and blood that revealed this to you but my Father in heaven" (16:17). Peter's declaration is the sign of readiness Jesus has been waiting for. In return for the identity his disciple has mirrored, Jesus reflects Simon's new identity. "You are 'Rock,' and on this rock I will build my church" (16:18), he says, promising him authority and indestructibility.

Both evangelists conclude their reports by stressing Jesus' charge not to reveal who he is outside the circle of the Twelve. They have become the privileged bearers of a truth too great yet to be borne by the people. The one who had called them from their homes, their families, their livelihoods was no less than the long-awaited Messiah.

They couldn't even begin to absorb it. But there it was, glimmering in their faces like the noonday sun. They could have no way of knowing how this revelation might brand them, burning away their former selves. After Caesarea Philippi, the disciples could never go home again.

Once they knew him, the die was cast.

MEDITATION

The day is young and innocent of oppressive schemes. Our pace is that of confident pilgrims whose travels have been marked by the sure signs of Yahweh's favor. By noon we hope to reach the villages outside Caesarea Philippi, the pagan stronghold of Herod's son. Who knows what reception awaits us! There's no room for worry among our recent memories of the crowds acclaiming Jesus, pressing towards him with open mouths as though he were a river and they'd been lost in the Negeb. You don't have to be a Galilean to be drawn to our rabbi. Once the people in this region hear him speak and see what power he has to heal, they will understand why we have left our nets to follow him.

Peter's up ahead, probably talking Jesus' ear off about all the miraculous cures we've witnessed these past few weeks: the daughter of the Syro-Phoenician woman whose cleverness and constancy made the Master's eyes narrow with knowing appreciation; the deaf-mute whose ears were opened and whose tongue suddenly recalled its purpose. Oh, there's plenty for Peter to exclaim about.

John's walking along at a distance behind the rabbi, always listening and watching—like an artist trying to see his subject in just the right light. The rest of us are taking our time, enjoying the perfume of the orange trees and the freedom of the day. We are content with our lot. Even though we have no provisions and our night's lodging will depend on some unknown host's generosity, why should we be anxious? Haven't we seen Jesus satisfy a sea of hungry people with an armful of bread and fish? Believe me, today we are like children whose father is so wealthy that we never have to waste time on such foolish cares.

Caesarea Philippi—the name rings with Roman pomposity. As though Augustus Caesar and Herod Philip were themselves gods to be worshiped in public places! But the town can't be blamed for the vanity of its overlord. In fact, we harbor an affection for this place on the slopes of Mt. Hermon where the Jordan begins its plunge southward to the sea. In this maternal river many of us, even Jesus himself, were baptized by John, that wild man of God whose voice made sinners tremble and the righteous fall on their knees. For us, the Jordan sings of Yahweh's splendor, his eternal majesty:

> Yahweh, the rivers raise,
> the rivers raise their voices,
> the rivers raise their thunders;
>
> greater than the voice of the ocean,
> transcending the waves of the sea,

> Yahweh reigns transcendent in the heights. *

One of the outlying villages is in sight now. We will welcome the chance to get off our feet for a while and rest in some haven of shade. James and Thomas are going ahead to greet the local people, to let them know that Jesus is coming. Maybe they will drum up a crowd for this afternoon. If we're lucky, they will find some good-hearted women to provide us with a jug of cool water, fresh bread, even a basket of figs.

There are women like that wherever we go. They've heard about Jesus, and even if they think he's too good to be true, they want to find out for themselves. When he speaks, they cradle his words, holding them like cherished infants to their hearts. He misses none of this, of course, and loves them for it.

"We can rest here," Peter calls back over his shoulder. His voice is always larger than it needs to be, a consequence of growing up on his father's fishing boats and learning to outshout the wind and the waves. He's a brusque man, all right. But he's as honest as homespun and straightforward to a fault. We never have to guess what Peter's thinking; it all tumbles out of him, pell-mell, like herring from an overloaded net. You never have to wonder where you stand with Peter. That's one of the things we like about him.

We've settled ourselves in a small almond grove. Jesus has already taken off his sandals and is stretched out on the warm earth, relaxing every muscle, relishing the first moments of ease after long exertion. His forehead glistens with sweat, but he makes no move to wipe it. When he rests, he is all at rest. It's a quality of his several of us have noticed—and envied: the ability to do just one thing at a time. I've never seen him make any of those nervous gestures we all have—no twirling of the beard, no tapping of the fingers or shifting from one foot to the other. If he's faced with some frustration or even danger, he stands there and lets it pass through him, as though he were somehow taking

*Psalm 93:3-4, *Jerusalem Bible.*

the sting out of it by refusing evasion. Who knows how he does it?

The scouts are back, laden with supplies. "We have friends here," James announces, taking pleasure in the prompt response Jesus' name evokes in towns where we might expect to be treated like strangers. "It seems there were some visitors from Caesarea Philippi in Bethsaida when Jesus cured that blind man a few days ago. They're spreading the word right now among their friends and relatives. Don't worry, Rabbi. We'll have a crowd for you by this afternoon." Jesus smiles lazily in James's direction. The fanning of the slender almond leaves pleases him; he observes them with an expression of esteem.

Andrew lays out the food and apportions the water for washing and drinking. We rotate these tasks so no one feels put upon and no one can become too self-important for domestic responsibilities. It was Peter's idea—and it didn't hurt his stature in Jesus' eyes. When it comes to the blessing, we leave that to the rabbi. To hear him pray is to understand—maybe for the first time—the meaning of the *shemá*: "…[Y]ou shall love the LORD your God, with all your heart, and with all your soul, and with all your strength."*

His prayer is never passive nor hollow. He inhabits it as fully as he inhabits his own body. It's as though he could see Yahweh enthroned right before his eyes. Even here under the almond trees, he prays with a devotion few synagogues ever witness. And, believe it or not, his prayer does something to the food. The goodness of the one gets into the other. It sounds silly, but when you close your teeth on that first mouthful of bread, you know it's true.

We bow our heads, and let his prayer nourish us:

> Father, we praise you for filling the well,
> for watering the fig tree,
> for ripening the grain.

*Deuteronomy 6:5, part of the daily prayer of pious Jews.

You are the source of our life
and the slaking of our thirst.
Nourish the seed of gratitude in our hearts
that we may continue to praise you
forever and ever.
Amen, Abba, amen.

Laughter and good spirits season the meal today. We're full of stories to swap, stories of how people have reacted to Jesus' teaching and healing. To tell the truth, we aren't sure what to make of it all ourselves. We've been on the road so much and so many things have happened that we're like newlyweds who receive too many presents at once. It's been miracle upon miracle. Maybe we're afraid to know what it adds up to.

Sometimes by the night fire, when the crowds have gone and Jesus has left us to find some solitary place to pray, we've talked about it—where we are going and who it is who leads us there. But, frankly, who wants to give the ultimate answer? What if we're wrong? When a dream has been tended by an entire nation for patient centuries, you don't go jumping to conclusions and shouting, "He's come! The Savior is here at last!" Even though we've done some pretty strange things in order to follow Jesus, we're still rational men, you can be sure. So we find it safer to skirt this question, hoping that Jesus will appease our curiosity when he's ready.

Right now such serious questions do not concern us. We're done with traveling for the day, and the townspeople will be awhile in coming out. The sun induces a soothing languor. Andrew is repairing his sandal, but everyone else seems fully occupied in lolling about on the stone wall or under the trees. John sings the first few measures of a common folk song, and his reedy voice is soon trampled on by the runaway baritones of Matthew, Thomas and James. The goodness of God resides in the almond grove like a provident wife enjoying her offspring.

Laughing at the spectacle of their own voices, the four begin insulting and jostling one another with boyish humor.

Although Jesus sometimes joins them in such roughhousing, today he is the older brother who smiles indulgently at the adolescent rowdies.

"What do you think of these camel-callers, Master? Have your ears ever been assaulted by music such as this before?" Peter wants to know.

"They rival the raucous crows," Jesus responds, looking at the quartet in a way that both affirms and quiets them. As always, it is John who first perceives the message in the rabbi's tone and posture. He leaves the others and sits cross-legged on the ground next to Jesus, having heard an invitation that the rest of us missed.

But we aren't donkeys, after all. We may not understand everything about Jesus—who could?—yet, we know enough to honor him with our attention at times like this. The Teacher doesn't waste words. He's like a wise farmer who never drains his well. He pours out just enough water for the seeds to germinate and take root. (Some of us are inclined to empty our buckets all at once.) So when Jesus speaks, we listen. If we didn't, we wouldn't be hanging around outside a pagan city in the middle of the day waiting for a young carpenter from Nazareth to tell us which end is up.

Jesus is propped up on his elbow, watching us as we come in closer. He's a mystery, you know. To look at him, you'd never suspect what authority dwells within that humble Galilean lodging. He could be a farmer or a shepherd. Frankly, he's not sturdy enough to earn his living on the lake. Don't get me wrong: In many ways, he's the strongest man I've ever met. But that slender frame and that face on which so many thoughts are written—you'd never mistake him for a brother to the Sons of Thunder!

"Who do people say that I am?"

His question surprises us. The rabbi is not the kind of person who broods over the opinion of others or seeks flattery in any guise. He observes us with a hart's wariness, however, as though he has a keen interest in whatever our next move might

13

be. This could be the opening we've been looking for.

"Some say you are John the Baptist come back to complete your mission," Matthew offers. Several disciples nod their heads. A few may have entertained that conjecture themselves back in the beginning.

"Others think you are Elijah. They say you will reveal Yahweh's plan to restore the Chosen People to their rightful prominence," says Thomas, separating himself from such a view by adopting a skeptical tone. Philip adds, "I've heard many people insist that you are one of the prophets, but greater than all those who have gone before you." Again, heads nod and a chorus of "yes, that's right" and "I've heard that, too" underscores the opinion.

During this exchange Jesus has been listening with a careful regard, looking up now and then from the almond leaf cupped in his hand. He makes no comment, but his expression assures us that he's missed nothing. What now? We've said our piece. An agreeable silence descends on the grove. He has taught us to be at home with silence, so we feel no uneasiness. Time is of no more consequence than a field full of cockle and doves' dung.

Jesus closes his palm, embracing the almond memento. His body shifts subtly toward us and the force of his expectancy startles us. He looks from one to the other of our faces with the expression of a suitor who can not hide his urgency. His sudden need makes us feel inadequate.

"But you," he says, acknowledging our intimate status, "who do you say that I am?"

The silence this time is a huge bird poised on a cliff, awaiting a favorable current before bursting into flight. We all want to answer. Yet we dread the pain—his and ours—if we are wrong about the dream. He has not taken his eyes from ours. The answer must be given now or the bird will never fly again.

"You are the Messiah!"

Thank God for Peter! He said it as confidently as he would his own name. He dared to speak in the daylight what we have whispered in our hearts at night. *The Messiah. The Savior. The Promised One.* What joy to liberate these words from fear's confinement: *The Messiah.* No name tastes sweeter in the mouth of an Israelite. And Peter has found the courage to give it to our Teacher, Jesus of Nazareth, Yeshua bar Joseph, the one who has called us to risk everything. And maybe gain all.

What I wouldn't do to be Peter at this moment! Look at the big galoot, soaking up every ounce of that magnificent smile Jesus has focused on him, as though the rest of us didn't need the sunshine as well. Despite his occasional swaggering and bullheadedness, Peter manages to come through with his hero's mantle swirling when it really counts.

I tell you, it's impossible to look at Jesus' face without getting lost in the sea of your own emotions. You'd think his fondest prayer had just been answered. He has taken Peter by the shoulders in a gesture so affectionate that it makes your throat ache to see it. "You're a happy man, Simon bar Jonah!" he says, shaking the beaming fisherman. "Only my Father in heaven could have revealed this to you."

Who can resist the two of them, standing waist-deep in a pool of happiness? The rest of us wade right in to join Peter, who has embarked on a greater sea voyage than any of us has ever imagined. We encircle disciple and Master, linking our arms, feeling the blood of Abraham and Jacob pulsing within us. The Messiah, the Messiah! We are rapidly getting drunk on the beauty of it. Someone raises the ancient psalm and we join in, creating a torrent of praise as we dance around and around, losing our heads in the impulsive joy of recognition.

> O God, with your judgment endow the king,
>> and with your justice, the king's son;
> He shall govern your people with justice
>> and your afflicted ones with judgment.
> The mountains shall yield peace for the people,
>> and the hills justice.
> He shall defend the afflicted among the people,

save the children of the poor,
and crush the oppressor.

May he endure as long as the sun,
and like the moon through all generations.
He shall be like rain coming down on the meadow,
like showers watering the earth.
Justice shall flower in his days,
and profound peace, till the moon be no more....

Blessed be the LORD, the God of Israel,
who alone does wondrous deeds.
And blessed forever be his glorious name;
may the whole earth be filled with his glory.
Amen. Amen. *

(Pause for at least five or 10 minutes of reflection on the Christ-event you have just participated in.)

AS THE DISCIPLES continue their celebration, find a quiet place on the slopes of Hermon at a little distance from the almond grove. Preserve the reflective spirit of your Gospel meditation. If distractions intrude, slowly and peacefully repeat the name of Jesus until you are again in focus.

Like Peter, you must respond to Jesus' question. The answer must emerge from your life: past, present, anticipated future. To give someone else's answer would be to disappoint the Teacher. Prepare yourself by considering these or other relevant questions that may come to you:

When I was a child, who was Jesus to me?

*Psalm 72:1-7, 18-19.

16

During my high school years, how did my relationship with Jesus change?

As a young adult, when I was choosing my life's course, what was my image of Jesus and how did it influence my choices—if at all?

When I consider the most important moments of my life (great sadness or joy, crucial change or danger, major achievement or loss), who was Jesus to me then?

Do I see any progression in the names and titles I have assigned to Jesus over the years? Do they reflect more about me than about him?

At this stage of my faith journey, who is Jesus to me?

What difference does he make in my life?

How am I making his identity known to others?

Give the Spirit time to bring all your answers together. If you are not yet ready to respond to Jesus, resolve to pray over this question for the next several days. When you are ready not only to respond but to make a continuing commitment to increase your understanding of Jesus' identity, go back to the almond grove where he is waiting for you.

"But you," he says, "who do you say that I am?"

CONCLUDING PRAYER

You are Son of the Most High,
> brother of the lowest.
You are God-Hero,
> and Mother-Courage.

You are open door and
         guest at table.
You are sturdy boat
         and swirling sea.
You are dwelling place and
         final destination.
You are still point
         and revolving planet.
You are single Word,
         cell of silence.

You are wilderness journey,
         desert tent;
         Lion of Judah,
         Lamb of Galilee;
         wine of Cana,
         water of Shechem;
         fig tree of Bethany,
         olive of Kidron;
         sign of Jonah,
         Temple of Jerusalem.

You are daily bread and boundless hunger;
         love given and love received;
         presence and promise;
         life and life-after;
         breath,
         sight,
         salt,
         gate,
         all.

Amen. Alleluia!

CHAPTER TWO

WHAT DO YOU WANT ME TO DO FOR YOU?

Jesus halted and ordered that he [the blind beggar] be brought to him. When he had come close, Jesus asked him, "What do you want me to do for you?" "Lord," he answered, "I want to see." Jesus said to him, "Receive your sight. Your faith has healed you." At that very moment he was given his sight and began to follow him, giving God the glory. All the people witnessed it and they too gave praise to God. (Luke 18:40-43)

WHEN THE TWO OLD MEN, fallen from power, meet in the fields of Dover in Shakespeare's *King Lear,* the one who has lost his sanity says to the other, robbed of his sight: "A man may see how this world goes with no eyes. Look with thine ears...." Lear, through his own willful blindness to flattery's deception, has been driven mad by two conniving daughters. His friend, the Earl of Gloucester, has been duped by an ambitious son, his eyes gouged out by the son's accomplice.

In the course of the play, both men move from blindness to insight. When an onlooker says to the unsteady Gloucester, "You cannot see your way," the ready response from the Earl is, "I have no way and therefore want no eyes; I stumbled when I saw."

Stories of the blind who see pervade the Gospels like the fragrance of Lebanese cedar. The evangelists often juxtapose a physical healing of blindness with an unmistakable example of spiritual blindness either in the disciples or in the religious authorities. As John tells the story of the man born blind (9:1-41), the recurring interplay between the blind who see and the seeing who are blind borders on slapstick comedy.

First, the disciples want to know what awful sin the man or his parents have committed. Once Jesus straightens them out on that point (the man's blindness is an opportunity to show forth God's work), he has to deal with the nearsightedness of the Pharisees. Their ploys to disprove the healing—drilling the man and his parents with obtuse questions, refusing to believe that Jesus healed by the power of God—are laughable to us. But their obstinate rejection of the truth is also tragic.

Welcoming the once-blind man as his disciple, Jesus says,

> "I came into this world to divide it,
> to make the sightless see
> and the seeing blind." (John 9:39)

When the Pharisees take offense at this barb, they are promptly knocked off their perches with:

> "If you were blind
> there would be no sin in that.
> 'But we see,' you say,
> and your sin remains." (John 9:41)

Unlike Gloucester, the Pharisees have neither the sense nor the insight to recognize that they stumbled when they saw.

Luke, Matthew and Mark give us three variations on the same theme when they describe what happened near Jericho as Jesus was on his way to Jerusalem. Each contrasts the healing incident with a manifestation of spiritual blindness. Luke directly precedes his account with the disciples' failure to understand Jesus' prediction of his death and rising. "His utterance remained obscure to them, and they did not grasp his meaning" (Luke 18:34b). Matthew contrasts his healing story with the dimness of those disciples who hanker after personal glory. When the mother of James and John wants a guarantee that her boys will be honored in the Kingdom, Jesus says that suffering and servitude come first. Mark presents James and John doing their own wheedling, but the result is the same.

As Matthew narrates the healing (20:29-34), there are *two* blind men sitting by the roadside when the crowd, following Jesus out of the city, engulfs them. Sensing their opportunity, they shout plaintively, "Lord, Son of David, have pity on us!" The crowd, intent on keeping Jesus' attention for its own purposes, attempts to silence them. But the blind men shout all the louder, "Lord, open our eyes!"

The physically blind had an in with Jesus. If they believed in his ability to heal them, he could no more pass them by than he could refuse bread to the starving. Their deprivation plucked at the harp strings of his compassion; their darkness begged at the gates of his mercy. The one who could see with excruciating clarity the beauty of his Father's artistry—the scarlet carpet of anemones, the spreading green bay tree, the gold apricots and the crimson rose of Sharon—could not bear that others should miss it. With a touch, Jesus unseals their vision and they follow after him.

According to Mark (10:46-52), a blind man named Bartimaeus competes with the crowd for Jesus' attention. Doing a humorous about-face, the people first scold Bartimaeus then—after Jesus has called him out of the crowd—urge him forward with solicitous reassurances. Ignoring their duplicity, the blind man throws off his cloak, bounds to his feet and lurches toward the sound of Jesus' voice. "Rabboni, I want to see," he insists. And the Lord responds, meeting sure faith with instant healing.

Luke's version (18:35-43) has the blind man, begging by the roadside, stop Jesus in his tracks with urgent shouting that is music to the rabbi's ears. Emerging from the dark, the beggar wobbles like a wine-sated reveler and opens his crusty eyes to see the face of Christ right there before him. He is overcome with gratitude and carries the crowd along with him in a cascade of praise.

Despite their differences, the stories harmonize on the theme of blindness banished and discipleship embraced. The blind do not pause to speculate about whether Jesus can heal them or not. They do not pander to their fears (What if he can't help me? What if my hopes are squashed? What if people think I'm a fool for believing in this man?). They trust in Jesus. No questions asked.

In Calvin Miller's poetic narrative *The Singer*, a miller with a crippled hand invites a young stranger to have supper with him. The stranger expresses his concern over the host's handicap and promises that he can make the hand useful again if the miller "will just desire it whole and believe it can be." But the self-pitying host scorns the Singer's promise. He wallows in the distinction of his pain. "The season of my hope is gone," he observes, expecting a rush of pity from his guest. Overhearing the miller's faithless prayer ("Oh, God deliver me from this body....I never can be well and whole as other men"), the Singer leaves him to his misery.

The blind men at Jericho can see more clearly than the miller with his mangled hopes. Their faith in Jesus as the Messiah is reflected back to them in healing love. This is no passive exchange, but a passionate sequence of actions verbalized as, "I trust. I believe. I see. I follow." Being a disciple may well involve more hardships than they have known as blind beggars. But that possibility does not give them a moment's pause. They throw themselves at Jesus, eager to accept whatever comes of believing in him.

Did the once-blind later know scorn and rejection? Did they discover that traveling with the Son of David wasn't all manna and honey? Did they, like the disciples at Emmaus, know the dizzying joy of seeing the risen Lord? To say "Lord, that I may see" is to make no idle request.

When Luke's blind man at Jericho heard Jesus asking "What do you want me to do for you?" he knew there was more to the question than met the ear. But, still blindfolded, he plunged right in, not knowing whether he would be crushed at the foot of craggy Sinai or refreshed in the brilliant blue Jordan.

MEDITATION

We are like those whose dreams are heavy with some vague foreboding, but whose days belie the nocturnal portents. Just yesterday, for instance—what a sight! Jesus was surrounded by children of every sort. There was no keeping them away. (We tried to fend them off, of course, but the rabbi insisted on allowing them to climb all over him.) For an unmarried man, he's unbelievably attracted to the little ones.

They hold his hands and tug on his beard, twirl the damp tendrils of hair over his ears, step on his toes and sit on his lap. One toddler, with black braids as long as she was, kept kissing him on the cheek and patting him on the shoulder in a motherly fashion. Jesus was right in his glory, I can tell you. He hugged them and listened to their quaint stories and laughed roundly at their innocent jokes. The mothers sat back in the shade, enjoying their leisure, secure in the affection our rabbi was so prodigally spending on their children.

Later in the day Peter had occasion to remind Jesus that we had left everything in order to become his followers. A rich young man had just left us after questioning the rabbi about how to attain everlasting life. At the sound of "Sell all you have and give to the poor,"* the rich man shrunk back as though Jesus had raised a hand to him. Then he fell into a melancholy state and walked away, deflated by his inability to accept the terms. We felt sorry for him, remembering the modest weight of our few possessions and worldly aspirations. After the man was out of earshot, Jesus reminded us that we would receive a plentiful return for having invested our trust in him.

We were still wandering in the mist of our rosy expectations when Jesus drew us aside for one of those private

* Luke 18:22.

23

revelations that have become more frequent lately. His strange prophecies soon turned our mist to somber gray. I promptly forgot as much of it as I could, hating the gloomy look in his eyes and the flat tone of his voice. He was predicting his death, but we would have none of it. We closed our minds to it, not allowing our idyllic life with him to be jeopardized by the fearful prospects his warning raised.

Now we are on our way to the Holy City by way of the Jordan Valley and the hallowed city of Jericho. Who can hear the name of Jericho and not be stirred by national pride? This great walled city, guarding the entrance to the Promised Land, was wrested from the Canaanites by the cunning of Joshua and the intervention of Yahweh. When you approach the city, you can almost hear the blood-chilling shouts of the invading Israelites, the moaning of the great rams' horns and the deafening rumble of the toppling walls. We can still taste the ancestral victory as the palms girding the city rise in the distance. Soon we'll wash the grime from our faces and cool our throats at the spring. We'll leave the dust devils behind and be comforted at the bosom of flourishing Jericho.

Andrew and Thomas have picked up the pace, urged on by the sight of the gates and the probability of hearing the latest gossip from travelers at the spring. If the truth be told, they're just as eager to indulge in gossiping themselves. Jesus' reputation has been spreading like a well-tended grapevine, and we aren't slow to identify ourselves as his chosen companions, the ones he plucked out of the ordinary run of things to be his witnesses and emissaries. In a friendly crowd, our stature grows by several cubits.

The men give us a slightly envious once-over, wondering, no doubt, how such common stock could have warranted the preference of so charismatic a leader. The women, on the other hand, can barely disguise their admiration, deducing that any friend of Jesus of Nazareth must be a person of uncommon worth. To the country youth, we are heroes; in the cities, the callow skeptics see us as buffoons.

"Here they come," Thomas announces, pointing out a small group of townspeople who seem to be a welcoming party. Jesus' shoulders straighten. He wipes his upper lip on his sleeve and shades his eyes, attempting to discern any familiar faces in the approaching company.

Excitement lightens our steps. Who knows what wonders the rabbi may perform today? Who can guess what wisdom, wrapped in homely metaphors, he will reveal? Or what if he raises the local hackles with his warnings against hypocrisy and corruption among those who wield authority? Life with Jesus keeps us on the edge, alert to the possibilities of conquest or defeat.

Their voices tumble over one another as they greet us. "Welcome, good rabbi." "Shalom, Yeshua bar Joseph." "So you've come to preach in Jericho at last?" "Will you stay with me and my family, Rabboni? My wife insists she must serve you and all your company." There are several merchants and elders and a few young artisans who want to see if Jesus will live up to his reputation. They aren't about to let him out of their sight now that he has arrived. In fact, they're elbowing one another, jousting for positions at Jesus' side as he strides along, accepting if not enjoying their clamorous recognition.

"Be quiet, beggar! Move aside." A portly wine merchant, scolding some poor person who remains invisible to us, is soon joined by others who brusquely order the importunate one to hush up if he knows what's good for him.

But as soon as they turn back to Jesus, vying for proximity to the holy man, a desperate voice cuts through the hubbub. "Jesus, Son of David, have pity on me!" The solid citizens are visibly offended at this intrusion on their private audience. "Son of David, have pity on me!" Before they can throttle him or have him dragged away, the beggar shouts again in a tone that half pleads, half demands.

Jesus stops in the middle of the road, raises a hand that silences the crowd as effectively as a thunderclap and asks who is calling him. It wouldn't matter if King Herod himself with all his

25

retinue appeared on the road at this moment. The rabbi wouldn't so much as give them a glance. That voice has riveted him to the beggar. "Bring him to me," he tells the elders, sensing their unwillingness to recognize the beggar as a brother and a person worthy of Jesus' attention.

Looking put upon, they fetch the beggar from the roadside. He's a sorry sight, I'll tell you, and the elders hold him at arms' length. His hair and beard are matted. His tunic needs a week's pounding and rinsing in the river. He's grasping an oak staff as though it were a treasure someone might wrest from him. His eyes stare vacantly and his head is wagging backwards at an awkward angle. He stumbles toward Jesus, more pushed than helped by the elders.

What a contrast the two of them make, standing in a circle cleared by the crowd: Jesus, straight as a cedar in the prime of his manhood. The blind man, bent and scraggly, undistinguished as a buckthorn. He's panting from the exertions of shouting and evading the clutches of the would-be silencers.

Jesus greets him not with pitying glances or solicitous words. That would be the way of many good people, those who would shake their heads over the beggar's misfortune and give him a few coins or a free meal. The rabbi studies the blind man the way some study their reflection in a pool. Where the rest of us see a stranger, Jesus seems to perceive someone closer in kinship to him right now than any of the rest of us.

"What do you want me to do for you?" He hasn't moved toward the blind man or touched him in any way. But that voice of his has reached out and embraced the beggar. There's no mistaking the compassion or the promise it holds.

The blind man straightens up, stretching his neck toward the voice like an eaglet looking to be fed. "Lord," he says, "I want to see."

It's as simple as that. He doesn't stammer or beg or cajole or flatter. He doesn't narrate his tale of hardship and woe to justify his right to be healed. He says the one thing that is necessary, confidently leaving the rest to Jesus.

26

"Receive your sight. Your faith has healed you," the rabbi tells him. He hasn't laid a finger on the man. But he has given him life as surely as a mother brings forth the child of her womb.

Immediately the beggar begins to vibrate with the onslaught of visual stimulation. He sways to the intoxicating rhythms of blue sky sailing over intense green palm branches, his virgin sight shrinking from its own incredible capacity. He is crooning a series of *aah*'s, his skinny arms reaching wildly for Jesus as the crowd presses in with a chorus of incredulous exclamations. "He can see! The old buzzard can actually see! Look at him! He's blinking and winking like some rosy-lipped maiden."

The blinking stops when he finds the face of his benefactor. He is a starving man suddenly confronted with a harvest feast. His eyes consume their fill, savoring the olive skin, the date-black eyes, the angular nose, the generous mouth curved in pleasure, the woolly beard to be tentatively stroked. "Ah!" he says again. "It's you." As though he'd known Jesus all along, known that he would give him sight, known that he would look just this way.

Then the new-sighted one throws his arms around Jesus, praising God with the vigor of an inspired cantor:

> Give to the LORD, you families of nations,
>   give to the LORD glory and praise;
>   give to the LORD the glory due his name! *

Carried on the wings of his exultation, we all join in, thanking the Lord for the great thing he has done in our midst. A procession forms as we move on toward Jericho. The new disciple follows at Jesus' heels, torn between keeping up with the Master and seeing everything in every direction at once.

His gratitude infects the rest of us. This is indeed "A land of wheat and barley, of vines and fig trees and pomegranates, a

* Psalm 96:7-8.

land of olive trees and honey."* We drink in the beauty of Jericho's lush oasis, alive with Yahweh's creative largesse. The faces of our fellow pilgrims are now more defined, more magnetic, more radiant.

I can't help wondering if the fervor of our latest disciple will survive our stay in the city. Will he still want to follow Jesus when the crowds are hostile and the Pharisees get up on their high pedestals to pepper us with scorn? Will he remain a pilgrim when we sleep in the fields on stormy nights and go hungry for a day or two? Will he thank God for his sight when he sees evil and greed and hatred in the faces of men and women?

Today he sees, inside and out. But what about tomorrow?

(Pause for at least five or 10 minutes of reflection on the Christ-event you have just participated in.)

WHILE THE DISCIPLES go on into Jericho, step aside from the procession and rest under a palm tree within sight of the well. Recall Jesus' question to the blind man: "What do you want me to do for you?"

Consider, in a relaxed and gradual manner, the potential implications of this question for you. Right now Jesus is sitting by the well. Before joining him, take time to work out what your response will be and how it will influence your present spirituality.

If Jesus offered to fulfill five dreams, wishes or prayers for me today, what would they be?

If only three, what would they be?

* Deuteronomy 8:8.

If only one?

What do my answers reveal about my present priorities?

Do I seem to have any blind spots in my expectations of Jesus?

As I review my daily prayer, what concerns, attitudes and desires recur most often?

In what ways do I most consistently practice the art of seeing? Do I have 20/20 vision when it comes to my own prejudices, my negative feelings about other people, my failures to form relationships in which I might be Christ for another?

Do I perceive the beauty and potential of the present, or am I frequently looking behind or ahead of where I am today?

Do I have eyes for what Graham Greene called the "moments and carriers of grace which are never what we expect them to be"?

Can I see beyond the cocoon of my immediate environment to the chronic suffering of political prisoners, cancer patients, refugees, the hard-rock poor and illiterate?

In what area of spiritual growth have I been most blind?

Allow the silence to hold you awhile longer. Jesus is a patient teacher, urgent only in his desire to see your eyes fully open to the light. When you are ready, go to the well. Behold the face that made the once blind man flounder, and hear him speak: "What do you want me to do for you?"

CONCLUDING PRAYER

Lord, that I may see:
> sense the brotherhood of soil,
>> the hopefulness of grass;
> detect the sportive ways of wind,
>> the companion songs of rain;
> observe the child's artless meditation,
>> the sculptor's rapt consideration;
> discern the stumbling stones to justice,
>> the manacles of law;
> apprehend the woman's hidden conflict,
>> the black man's dark defeats;
> contemplate my abject neighbor's deprivation,
>> my patient Teacher's expectation;
> perceive the Spirit's fire on the earth,
>> God's dwelling in my core.

Behold! You make all things new.
> You give sight to the blind.
> You reveal the oasis of truth.

Lord, that I may wholly seize and see all the way through.

CHAPTER THREE

WHY DO YOU CALL ME 'LORD, LORD'?

"A good man produces goodness from the good in his heart; an evil man produces evil out of his store of evil. Each man speaks from his heart's abundance. Why do you call me 'Lord, Lord,' and not put into practice what I teach you? Any man who desires to come to me will hear my words and put them into practice." (Luke 6:45-47)

THE EPISCOPAL PRIEST-AUTHOR Alan Jones once observed, "Sunday by Sunday people preserve themselves from an attack of serious Christianity by taking in a small amount." They are, he adds, like smallpox vaccination recipients who take a minor injection of the disease so as not to be overcome by the fullness of it. There should be no such thing, Jones implies, as a part-time, halfway, "sort of" Christian. "But because you are lukewarm, neither hot nor cold, I will spew you out of my mouth!" (Revelation 3:16)

We come-lately Christians can easily miss how strange and provocative Jesus was to the people of his day. He rarely did or said what was expected of him by the religious authorities, his own family or his disciples. He was the greatest spiritual provocateur the world has ever known.

But we who have been inoculated (via conventional religious education, comfortable Church membership, unexamined patterns of worship and service) rarely get agitated enough to respond to the Christ whose teaching uprooted people from their jobs and homes, wrested materialists from their greed and attachments, freed sinners from their weakness and self-indulgence.

In a semiconscious way, we may think we have reached a certain accommodation with Jesus by letting him rule specific areas of our lives. The disciples, when they were still wet behind the ears, deceived themselves in just that way. It was easy enough for them to focus on the glad tidings, the healings, the reinterpretation of the old Law. But once the Twelve had been named and taken aside for the Great Discourse (Luke's version of the Sermon on the Mount), the whitecaps began to mount up on the lake and the days of gentle sailing were over.

Chronologically, the Great Discourse precedes Peter's recognition of Jesus at Caesarea Philippi. Experientially, however, we are more apt to get hooked by Christ's conversion questions after we have answered, in an intensely personal way, who he is and what we are asking of him, the questions of the first two chapters.

"Why do you call me 'Lord, Lord'?" comes in the context of the great and greatly demanding discourse of Jesus to the disciples. In Matthew 5—7, it follows the Sermon on the Mount—the Beatitudes and the Golden Rule—delivered to the crowd gathered on the shore of the Sea of Galilee. There it takes the form of a declaration rather than a question: "None of those who cry out, 'Lord, Lord,' will enter the kingdom of God, but only the one who does the will of my Father in heaven" (Matthew 7:21).

Luke's Gospel, sometimes known as the "Gospel of absolute renouncement," records the scene on the Plain of Gennesareth (6:17-49). After spending the night on the mountain in prayer, Jesus is surrounded by people "from all Judea and Jerusalem and the coast of Tyre and Sidon." They have come to be instructed or healed or exorcised, and they all want to touch him. Power goes out from him. The lame dance, the mute sing, the possessed are free.

Then Jesus turns aside from the crowd and addresses his

disciples. To them (and us) he says,

> "Blest are you poor;
> the reign of God is yours...." (Luke 6:20)

The Beatitudes and their contrasting "woes" are followed by a
dynamic volley of instructions on how to love one's enemies. We
can only guess at the immediate reaction of the disciples. But to
picture them with mouths agape or vacant stares at the prospect
of blessing the Romans may not be far off the mark. (Matthew
says that the crowds were left spellbound at his teaching.)

Significantly, the Son of Man directs these difficult words
of counsel "to you who hear me" (Luke 6:27). He knows only too
well that if 50 disciples are listening, 15 may hear him. To those
whose heads are not covered by security blankets and self-defense
cloaks, Jesus speaks of turning the unstruck cheek, embracing the
enemy, lending without hope of a return. Instead of protecting
yourself with judgment and condemnation of others, he advises,
become proficient in pardoning without measure.

Why go to these herculean lengths of charity? The Master
uses a familiar image (payment in grain) to convey a highly
prodigal reward: "Good measure pressed down, shaken together,
running over, will they pour into the fold of your garment. For
the measure you measure with will be measured back to you"
(Luke 6:38).

The promise is as potent as the expectation that precedes
it. As a teacher who leads people forth, assuring them by his
confidence that they are capable of greater things than they have
yet attempted, Jesus has no parallel. Any listener whose heart
was open to the extravagance of the "good measure" image would
be ready to rise up on the spot and give his tunic to the nearest
beggar. (Recall the march to the sea to make salt or the
conflagration of English-made clothing in the movie *Gandhi* as
reminders of how powerful effective teaching can be.)

While the golden grain vision is still fresh, Jesus goes on to
a good tree. A tree is known by its fruit. And who wants to eat

33

decayed figs? So each person is identified by the words that blossom from his or her heart. If these words are evil or hypocritical, the heart is sick and needs healing. The virtue of sincerity—which we tend to discount, mistaking it for some sweet-smelling sentiment on a greeting card—is prized by the rabbi who repeatedly preached unity of heart, word and action. He heaped blazing "woes" on the heads of frauds and fakers.

So too the person who devotedly calls Jesus "Lord" and sits attentively at his feet is in big trouble if he or she then goes home to abuse the children or insult the neighbors. Once the Lord's words have been heard, not just sown in sparse soil, they must be given life. Otherwise, we become insincere witnesses to a false religion.

Jesus concludes with a neatly-constructed parable about how we build our houses (Luke 6:47-49). If we have no foundation in habitual practice, we will be swept away by the torrent of secular philosophy and self-serving goals. When we erect our homes on earthquake faults and sand dunes, we remain lords of our own lives as long as the sun shines.

But when the earth trembles and the sea pounds at our front door, there's a question waiting to be confronted: "Why do you call me 'Lord, Lord' and then go off and do your own thing?"

MEDITATION

I don't know about the others. There's been no time to talk things over, share a cup of wine, sit on some amiable host's roof where the breeze might clear our heads. The Twelve has had its initiation, I can tell you. Jesus had no sooner named us than he immersed us in a river of rabbinical teaching the likes of which we've never known.

He left no stone unturned, no assumption upright. Now he's ready to go on into Capernaum, fresh as an almond blossom in January, while the rest of us are as spent as if we'd lugged mud bricks in the sun all day. Will we ever be able to keep up with him? Not in any sense, I'm afraid.

My head is too cloudy to sort it all out. First, there was the exhilaration of being chosen from among all who had been following him since the death of the Baptizer. Jesus came down from the mountain, all fired up by his nightlong vigil. Like a long-distance runner, he had passed through several barriers of fatigue. But despite the darkness under his eyes, he was as refreshed as if he'd slept on a rich man's divan.

Anyway, the 12 of us were full of ourselves when he called us at daybreak. But the crowd was even at that hour gathering on the plain—streaming in from Judea and Jerusalem and the cities to the south—so we had little time for self-congratulation or pondering what our appointment might mean. Hospitality required us to greet the farmers and shepherds and fishermen and homemakers and weavers who had come out to see the wonder-working rabbi from Nazareth.

Several hours passed with Jesus going among the people in every section of that vast crowd. Once the healings began, they were all crazy to touch him—his hands, his face, his tunic, even his sandals. We went with him, trying as best we could to restrain them from gobbling him up in a fit of religious fervor. It wasn't easy. To be near him then was to be seared by the heat of his healing power. We were feeling pretty feverish ourselves!

Once he had satisfied their needs, did Jesus throw himself down on the ground to restore his energy with a barley loaf and a honeyed confection? Oh, no. While the people took their leisure, sharing whatever food the provident had brought along, the rabbi fed us on sterner staples. He told us what it meant to be a disciple. And it gave us pause, I'll tell you. Only a liar would say that it didn't make one wish—however temporarily—to be back home, safe in the harbor of a former life.

Jesus began by separating the flock. The poor from the rich, the hungry from the sated, the sorrowful from the revelers, the ostracized from the accepted. We had no trouble seeing ourselves as the good sheep, and we were eager to hear more "woes" to the powerful.

"To you who hear me, I say: Love your enemies, do good to those who hate you; bless those who curse you and pray for those who maltreat you."* That's what he said—do you believe it! I'll never forget it. Those words were the signal that the tide had turned. We were going to have to take some rough water ourselves. Being good sheep was just the beginning, it seems. If we wanted to live up to Jesus' expectations, we had to pet the Roman wolves, befriend the Samaritan aliens, pray for the tax collector who cheated us.

I remember Peter scowling up a storm as the impact hit him. He even stood up, probably with the full intention of setting Jesus straight on the practical side of life. But the rabbi never even took notice of him. He was speaking with a single-mindedness learned from his prayer. He knew we'd be confused and confounded by his teaching. He gave us credit, however, for our goodwill and trust. His face glowed as though the words coming out of his mouth were made of light.

The discourse went on, sweeping us along with its moral force. I can't retrieve its entire scope right now. My sense of fairness was provoked by Jesus' insistence that we lend without looking for a return. Won't that make us the easy prey of the jackals and the laughingstock of the villagers? Not only that. We are to pardon our enemies, no matter what the offense, and give up our accustomed role as judges of our persecutors, our betters and our pariahs. The rabbi's critics will rub their hands in glee when they get hold of this.

And what if we should attempt these supernatural heights of human perfection? That was the part Jesus was most eager to disclose. His voice deepened. His arms made wide gestures of gathering. He smiled at us with the pleasure of a vineyard owner surveying an excellent crop. It was as though we'd already accomplished all that he had asked in his Father's name. He saw our reward with eyes that could lay hold of the future and make it immediate.

* Luke 6:28.

36

"Give and it shall be given to you,"* he said. What a picture he then etched in our imaginations! Bundles of gold (whether finest wheat, purest gold or greater treasure, we didn't define) spilling into our folded tunics, filling, falling over, covering our feet, mounting in a glorious heap around us. Those who could be profligate with their forgiveness would be recompensed in a manner so generous that it made our heads whirl to consider it.

If Jesus had only stopped there. But you won't be surprised to learn that he didn't tarry on that plateau. He kept right on climbing, dragging us with him, whether we wanted to go or not. We were warned against being—or following—blind guides whose destination is the loathsome pit of destruction.

Then his voice took on a keener edge that made us squirm a little. "Why look at the speck in your brother's eye when you miss the plank in your own?"† Jesus asked. None of us dared look at another. We are, after all, one with the common run of folks who are better at discerning how others have gone wrong than at seeing our own detours. "Hypocrites!" he said, and I saw John and Matthew flinch, undoubtedly for different reasons.

If there is one thing the rabbi can't abide, it's duplicity. Because he is always what he seems to be, he expects others to be equally genuine. He knows deception is rooted in us from our youth. Yet he wants us, now that we are men (or women, for that matter) to work at achieving a harmony between the inner and outer self.

Anyway, he compared us to trees, reminding us that a good date palm doesn't produce decayed fruit. "A good man produces goodness from the good in his heart; an evil man produces evil out of his store of evil," he warned. Although I consider myself a good man, I had no trouble calling to mind several negative things that have issued from my storehouse lately. I had, for instance, belittled a tax collector whose fat, greasy face and despicable profession offended me. He had sought a private word

* Luke 6:38.   † Luke 6:41.

37

with Jesus and when he tried to slip me a few coins, I pushed him away with harsh insults. The recollection shamed me.

Jesus paused, allowing us to reflect, as much as we dared, on the nature of our heart's abundance. He just stood there in front of us until his silence became more unsettling than his discourse. Then, in an expression of concern rather than correction, he asked, "Why do you call me 'Lord, Lord,' and not put into practice what I teach you?"

The honesty of it knocked me back on my haunches. The truth hurt. I remember blinking rapidly to avoid the possible disgrace of tears. Peter bowed his head and coughed unnecessarily. Thomas looked as though someone had struck him. Several others shifted their weight, averting their faces from direct encounter with the rabbi. Only John looked directly at Jesus with unqualified admiration. How could the Teacher be so stunningly accurate, so painfully simple? No word eased the tension.

Why do we who love Jesus more than any other, who respect and cherish his words, who have cast our lot with him and pledged our lives to him, why do we so often revert to our old ways? Why is it so difficult to remember his teaching at the times when we most need it? Why do we do or say what we don't really intend? Why does the goodness in our hearts sometimes turn sour on its way to the surface? Why do our relentless tongues betray our best intentions?

Oh, there are answers. Some of them valid. Habit, provocation, forgetfulness, evil example, exhaustion, insecurity, conformity, revenge, self-defense—I could go on. But what's the point? There's not a one of those answers I'd hold up to Jesus. He'd see right through it. What's worse, he'd see through me and I'd have to come to terms with my wrongheadedness. That can't be done in a day. But the rabbi clearly wants us to start walking briskly in the right direction without delay.

While we were sitting there in various states of stupor, perplexity and reflection, Jesus decided to bring us out of it with a parable. It served two purposes, as his stories always do. First, it presented us with a familiar picture, a humorous one that prompted us to laugh at the donkey who put up his house without a foundation. The poor oaf probably stood there scratching his head while his roof caved in and the brick walls went careening away with the torrent.

But the story also gave us a chance to respond to Jesus' question. Not by giving excuses for our former ways, but by deciding to change—with his help. To do all we could to evict hypocrisy from our hearts, to become hearers who do the Word of God—and to begin today: that was what he asked of us.

The great discourse was over. He had given us enough to chew on into our old age. As we stood up, he embraced each one of us like a kindhearted general who knows his soldiers face overwhelming odds. When he held me briefly by the shoulders, shame was ousted and I knew I would cross the Negeb without water for him if he asked me. He must have felt the flame of my idealism, because he laughed and said reassuringly, "I believe you."

Then, when we wanted to stay together on the plain, Jesus picked up his staff, shook the dust from his tunic and strode off in the direction of Capernaum. "Come on," he urged over his shoulder. "They're waiting for us."

(Pause for at least five or 10 minutes of reflection on the Christ-event you have just participated in.)

STAY ON THE GRASSY PLAIN, knowing you can later rejoin Jesus and the others in the city. You have the advantage the Twelve disciples desired: time to consider the question that unsettled them. Take it apart and see how it applies to you.

Why do I call Jesus "Lord"?

Does the title, as I use it, imply that he is God and Master?

If I say that Jesus is God and King, Lord and Master, what does that mean in terms of how I relate to others, determine personal values, set goals, spend time, pray and worship? (Recall your well-considered answer to "Who do you say I am?")

If Jesus is the Lord of my life, what prevents me from putting his teaching into practice?

Select one teaching—one word from Jesus—that you often have trouble with. For example:

> "Lend without expecting repayment" (Luke 6:35).
>
> "...[E]veryone who grows angry with his [or her] brother will be liable to judgment..." (Matthew 5:22).
>
> "Should anyone press you into service for one mile, go with him two miles" (Matthew 5:41).
>
> "If you want to avoid judgment, avoid passing judgment" (Matthew 7:1).
>
> "Say, 'Yes' when you mean 'Yes' and 'No' when you mean 'No'" (Matthew 5:37).

Recall your most recent difficulty in adhering to this word. Picture what actually happened. Can you see what blinded you to your opportunity to generate goodness in a negative situation? Recall the disciple's speculation on what those blinders might be. Do any of his suggestions apply? If the Lord himself asked you to come up with a more positive and creative way of handling the situation, what would your response be?

Knowing that you can reasonably work on a single area of "putting into practice" at one time, decide which area it will be. Make a commitment to begin *today* and to continue applying yourself to it until measurable results have been achieved.

Keep some form of written record over a period of weeks. A

desk calendar, a journal or a chart of your own devising will enable you to see—either by brief notations or extended reflections—what's actually happening in a spiritual area that you may have been hiding under the rug. The record itself will motivate visible progress.

If it seems right to you, seal your commitment today with an act that verifies your sincerity in calling Jesus "Lord."

Go ahead into Capernaum to find the Teacher. When you have responded to his question, listen again to the terms of your relationship with him: "Any person who desires to come to me will hear my words and put them into practice."

CONCLUDING PRAYER

If I call you "Sir,"
> do I imply respect wrapped in gentle courtesy?

If I call you "Master,"
> am I bound to be your obedient and ready servant?

If I call you "Messiah,"
> do I pledge my faith that you are salvation's path?

If I call you "Christ,"
> am I recognizing your anointed right to guide me?

And if I name you "Lord,"
> do I swear that your word will blossom from my storehouse?

May my house be founded on your wisdom.
May my intention be verified in act.
May my life proclaim you
Lord,
Lord.

CHAPTER FOUR

WHO ARE MY MOTHER AND MY BROTHERS?

> The crowd seated around him told him, "Your mother
> and your brothers and sisters are outside asking for you."
> He said in reply, "Who are my mother and my brothers?"
> And gazing around him at those seated in the circle he
> continued, "These are my mother and my brothers.
> Whoever does the will of God is brother and sister and
> mother to me." (Mark 3:32-35)

NIKOS KAZANTZAKIS shocked Christians out of their pews
in 1960 when he published his unorthodox novel, *The Last
Temptation of Christ.* The protagonist wages a constant battle
against temptation in every guise—not only the seductive
temptations that allure all men and women but the temptation to
be only human, to deny his identity as the Father's beloved Son.
Until Jesus finally accepts his identity, Kazantzakis calls him "the
son of Mary."

Catholics whose image of Mary requires her to be a
constantly devoted and understanding mother might well be
provoked by the novelist's vision of her. Although she is a good
mother with great hopes for her son, the years of suffering his
eccentric, God-haunted behavior have prodded her close to
despair. She accuses God, asking, "Why did you cast your
thunderbolt and plant in my womb this daydreamer, this night-
walker of an only son?" She is distraught because Jesus brings her
neither the satisfactions of a normal son nor the joys of a divine
one.

After the son of Mary has plunged into his ministry, she tries to save him from the blows of an angry crowd by convincing them that Jesus is out of his senses. Then, taking his hand, she begs him to come home and be a respectable son. He responds, "I have no home. I have no mother. Who are you?" Mary weeps and speaks no more.

In the context of the novel, this is a heartrending scene—but no more so than the scene Mark portrays in the above reading. Many of us have tried to water it down, turn it around, do whatever is necessary to protect Jesus' reputation as a loving son. Those who think he is putting his family down or subordinating his relationship with them, we suppose, must be interpreting the passage too literally.

Biblical scholars, however, offer little support for that way out. As Raymond Brown *et al* in *Mary in the New Testament* observe, various attempts to soften the text or construe it in other ways don't stand up under analysis. Mark fully intends to define, in an incontestable fashion, the eschatalogical family of Jesus over against his natural family. He opposes those who are inside with Jesus to those who are outside. The point of the passage is not to exclude the mother and brothers and sisters (who may join the inner circle); it is to define the family that is "called into being by Jesus' proclamation of the Kingdom."

The reward of those who remain faithful to the eschatalogical (Kingdom) family is described later: Those who have given up their natural families for the sake of Jesus will receive "in this present age a hundred times as many homes, brothers and sisters, mothers and children and property—and persecution besides—and in the age to come, everlasting life" (Mark 10:30). Allegiance to the Lord must be thicker and stronger than blood.

This hard saying—"Who is my mother?"—follows directly after the choice of the apostles and the blasphemy of the scribes who charge that Jesus expels demons by the power of Beelzebul. As Mark tells the story, Jesus is staying in a house in Capernaum with his disciples. A crowd, excited by news of his miraculous healing power, fills the house, making the usual meal preparations impossible. Word of the charismatic gathering reaches Jesus' family and they set out to take charge of him for his own good. Their speculative accusation, "He is out of his mind" (Mark 3:21), is paired with the scribes' charge that he is possessed. Neither group understands Jesus or his actions.

The scene is set for the Lord to identify the primary basis of relationship with him. Whoever does the will of God, he says, is his closest kin. Whoever turns the other cheek to the persecutor, whoever seeks reconciliation with an offender before approaching the altar, whoever hears Jesus' word and puts it into practice, is "brother, sister and mother to me" (Mark 3:35).

Luke's version of this teaching is more maternal, less divisive. After reporting the blasphemy of the scribes, he tells us that a woman in the crowd calls out, "Blest is the womb that bore you and the breasts that nursed you!" The Lord gently turns that around to, "Rather, …blest are they who hear the word of God and keep it" (Luke 11:27,28).

That small but significant *rather* is what we deal with now.

MEDITATION

If another person squeezes through that door, we'll all be done for. There won't be enough air to go around. The oil lamp has already gone out and one old woman, in a dead faint, had to be hoisted over a battery of shoulders before she could be revived outside. I don't know why Jesus didn't have the foresight to go out in the courtyard when the first 25 or so people arrived. He stayed right here in the middle of the floor with concentric circles forming around him, layers of sitting, crouching, kneeling, standing, slumping, leaning humanity. I've been elbowed and stomped on so many times I'm ready to clobber the next oaf who so much as scowls in my direction.

Oh, for that cool breeze that kissed us on the mountain when Jesus called us to join him! But here we are, crammed together like rockfish in a net, gasping and writhing to survive. Our nostrils are assaulted by the odors of plentiful sweat, stale olive oil and musty grapes. It's midday, but only a madman would attempt to prepare a meal in this huge oven—even if someone had had the foresight to gather supplies from the neighbors. They're all babbling at once in here, but Jesus is no more perturbed than an aspen on a still day. He sits there in that little circle of serenity while all around him is in turmoil.

Things could be worse, I guess. The life of a disciple is no lamb's wool pillow. At least I'm near enough to the door to escape into the court. Not that I'd be out of the briarpatch even then. From what I can see, that space is rapidly being occupied by new arrivals—some from Jerusalem and others from Nazareth.

If those are scribes out there, there might be trouble. It was a mob scene yesterday when Jesus scared the evil spirits out of the possessed, while in ear-rending screeches they cried, "You are the Son of God!"* Jesus tried to shut them up, but plenty of people had already heard them.

"He is possessed by Beelzebul.... He expels demons with the help of the prince of demons."† That's Eleazar riling people up. That scribe's mouth is as big as his ambition. He's forever trying to establish himself as a leader, one whose opinions are worth their weight in myrrh. Jesus has to be wary of men like that. His authority threatens them and they'll have to strike back. I've passed the word along to Peter. Maybe we can avoid an outright confrontation.

I think I've just spotted Mary and several other relatives with the group that arrived from Nazareth. Jesus hasn't seen her since he left home. No doubt there'll be a festive reunion tonight if we can ever get rid of this crowd. How much does Mary know of the miracles Jesus has been performing? Of all Jewish mothers, she must ache with pride in such a son.

"We've come to take charge of him." That imperious voice carries clear across the courtyard. It's Samuel, one of Jesus' older

*Mark 3:11. † Mark 3:22.

cousins. He's angry and embarrassed about something. The others seem to be restraining him from going into the house. Now he's yelling, "He is out of his mind."*

That misguided do-gooder actually believes that Jesus is possessed. He's planning on dragging the Master away. Between the scribes and the relatives, where's the greater danger? One side wants to discredit and possibly destroy him. The other wants to put him away for his own good.

Jesus has summoned Eleazar and two other scribes in order to respond to their charges. He's standing, still serene, in the circle which is meticulously respected by the poor cobs who are only too happy to prance on each other's toes.

"How can Satan expel Satan?"† he asks, skewering the scribes on the spot. With perfect logic, he points out that neither a household nor a kingdom divided against itself can survive. Therefore, if Satan has mutinied against himself, he's done for. "I give you my word, every sin will be forgiven mankind and all the blasphemies men utter, but whoever blasphemes against the Holy Spirit will never be forgiven. He carries the guilt of his sin without end."‡

The scribes are speechless. His authority terrifies them. Had they, in truth, sinned against the Spirit by claiming that Jesus is possessed? Had their refusal to affirm his goodness been a greater evil than they knew? Eleazar's face is parchment stiff. He turns to follow the other two who have circumspectly made their way through the crowd.

"Your mother and your brothers are outside asking for you." A young woman has delivered the message, apparently unaware of Samuel's intentions. As I try to reach the inner circle to speak to Jesus (Who wants to see a family squabble in public?), he resumes his cross-legged position on the floor, flushed from his triumph over the scribes.

He looks around at the eager, hungry, devoted crowd, loving each one with a glance. Quiet descends on their

* Mark 3:21.   † Mark 3:23.   ‡ Mark 3:28-29.

shoulders. "Who are my mother and my brothers?" he asks. What a question! As though he didn't know the womb that carried him or the blood that courses in his veins. There's not a person in this house who wouldn't rather hear the answer than fill his growling stomach or empty a cup of cold goat's milk down his gullet right now.

"These are my mother and my brothers," he says. "Whoever does the will of God is brother and sister and mother to me." Time passes. His words slowly, slowly trickle down between the boulders of unknowing. Light dawns on one face, then another. Smiles of recognition are exchanged among those who have jostled and waited and sweated and starved together. Women embrace one another, while the men content themselves with slapping backs. Peter is beaming as though he'd said something astounding himself.

I can't help thinking of my own family back home in Nazareth. What would they think if Jesus' words reached their ears? Would they judge him a hardhearted, unnatural son of Abraham? If they were here at this moment, they'd know better. They'd understand that Jesus is neither belittling nor excluding them. They too can be members of this family gathered here today in Capernaum—or tomorrow in Gerasa, or next year in Jerusalem. They can, if they choose, join the family of those who hear and do the will of God as Jesus has revealed it to us.

As I see it, what Jesus is saying is this: Relationship with me is more than a matter of blood kinship and home and genealogy and geography. These things are good. But there is a higher good. Each of us is born not just into the family of Levi or the family of David. We are born into the family of God. We are the people who do God's work and who have been called to the Kingdom by Jesus of Nazareth, proclaimer of the Good News of our salvation.

What if there is a conflict between these two families, as there was for Jesus today? He answered that for us by remaining with us. When he was young, it was right for him to follow the will of Mary and his brothers. Now he is a man. The sword of division is unsheathed. We who are apostles have felt its blade. But the Kingdom requires us to rise above our ordinary selves.

We've left the comforts of home and family. Jesus has become our mother and father, our brother and sister, our home and hearth. Some have been tempted to turn back. But it wouldn't work even if all 12 of us returned to our old ways. The memory of Jesus would burn in our stomachs and simmer in our brains until we were driven like stampeding sheep to find him again.

We're far from perfect, mind you. But we do know who our mother is.

(Pause for at least five or 10 minutes of reflection on the Christ-event you have just participated in.)

AS THE CROWD is dispersing, climb the stone stairwell by the house. Sit or lie down on the roof to pray. Sort out what you have just seen and heard. Consider what meaning Jesus' rhetorical question and its response hold for you.

Have I almost always put my family first when it came to making important decisions? Observing the holidays? Gift-giving?

If not, when have I put the interest of others (or perhaps my own) before my family's concerns?

What criteria do I apply in determining whether or not my family takes precedence over others?

How do I feel about Jesus' question, "If you love those who love you, what credit is that to you? Even sinners love those who love them" (Luke 6:32)?

Do I feel the same way about "Who is my mother?"

Which is most unsettling to me and why?

Can I recall situations when I have been called on to put into practice the following: "Whoever loves father or mother, son or daughter, more than me is not worthy of me" (Matthew 10:37)?

Are there times when it is necessary to be at odds with my family in order to be faithful to Jesus?

Does my family seem to be part of the group inside the house at Capernaum or outside? If outside, is there anything I can do to draw them in? (Whatever I do must be based on knowledge of and respect for their present state. Witness speaks more effectively than preaching; happiness smells sweeter than self-righteousness; love leaves no room for judgment.)

Who are the people I have recognized as my "mother" and how have they influenced my spiritual life?

Are there others whom I have avoided because of natural differences or insecurities?

Jesus will soon come up on the roof to rest and spend some time with you. Be ready to enter into dialogue when he asks: "Who is your mother?"

CONCLUDING PRAYER

Oh, eminent slayer of sleek assumptions,
    enemy of stereotypical views,
Fire no more of your searing questions,

  withhold your provocative news.
You roust us from goosedown contentment,
  rob us of conventional good;
Your word leaves no stone untoppled,
  no familiar pattern of *should.*
If domestic blood is not thicker than spirit,
  hearth not higher than will,
Where shall God's Kingdom lead us?
  Are we sundered still?

CHAPTER FIVE

WHAT DOES IT PROFIT A PERSON...?

> "If a man wishes to come after me, he must deny his very
> self, take up his cross, and follow in my steps. Whoever
> would preserve his life will lose it, but whoever loses his
> life for my sake and the gospel's will preserve it. What
> profit does a man show who gains the whole world and
> destroys himself in the process? What can a man offer in
> exchange for his life? If anyone in this faithless and
> corrupt age is ashamed of me and my doctrine, the Son
> of Man will be ashamed of him when he comes with the
> holy angels in his Father's glory." (Mark 8:34-38)

IN THE AGE OF VICTORIA, an American Catholic woman
threw away a life of intellectual and material pleasures to lose
herself in one of the vilest slums New York City's Lower East
Side had to offer. A separation from her husband of 20 years,
well-to-do editor George Lathrop, had been sanctioned by the
Church at her request. Although husband and wife had been
converted to Catholicism at the same time, George's faith
remained lukewarm while Rose's prodded her to a larger
devotion. He became an alcoholic, she a seeker after meaning.
At 45 Rose Hawthorne Lathrop, daughter of Puritan novelist
Nathaniel Hawthorne, took the intrepid leap into the unknown.

Living alone in a condemned apartment, she began her
ministry among "the uncherished poor." The beautiful, fastidious
and once-imperious Rose of the drawing room became the

compassionate friend of poor, incurable cancer patients whose bodies were ravished by a disease that had no treatment. They were the lepers of their day, avoided by polite society and dumped in holding stations to die like cast-off pets. Rose nursed them, respected them and gave them back a sense of their self-worth. She lavished her care on them for 30 years founding, after her husband's death, a secular Dominican order known as the Servants of Relief of Incurable Cancer.

Long before Mother Teresa of Calcutta began tending the dying or Dame Cicely Saunders founded the Hospice movement, Rose provided thousands of cancer patients an opportunity to die with dignity in the embrace of Christ's Servants of Relief. Her life among Christ's poor imposed constant emotional and physical stress, rejection, depressing conditions, illness and the unrelenting pain of not being able to do enough. Rose Hawthrone Lathrop gave away all that most rational people consider desirable for what most people fear and avoid.

Shortly after Peter gave his inspired response at Caesarea Philippi, Jesus raised a specter—the shadow of the cross. He knew his students' limitations, so he prepared himself for a long haul of explanation, repetition and reiteration. His insistence that suffering must go before glory convinced many to seek a more congenial Messiah. His prediction that he would be put to death prompted Peter to take him aside for some fatherly advice.

"Look, Lord. You can't go around talking openly about defeat by the priests and scribes. Negativism is out. And dying? Now that's ridiculous! You won't win disciples that way, I can assure you. Nobody wants to follow a loser." That was the gist of Peter's worldly wisdom. And, had we been there, we might have added our Amens to his pragmatic advice. But what was Jesus' reaction? Did he thank Peter for his help? Commend him for his solicitude?

Mark informs us that he soundly reprimanded the disciple: "Get out of my sight, you satan! You are not judging by God's standards but by man's!" (Mark 8:33). We have to admire the effectiveness of the rebuke even while commiserating with Peter,

54

who felt like skulking away to crawl under a rock. Simon, a satan? The other disciples couldn't miss the implication of Jesus' vehemence. The doctrine of the cross might not be understood right away, yet it had better not be rebutted by anyone calling himself or herself a disciple.

What Mark presents as a single discourse (8:34-38) is more likely a compilation of fine-cut sayings that effectively reinforce one another. These "commitment sayings" dash the hopes of any disciple who intends to coast into the Kingdom on a reputation for conventional goodness. Being kind to one's friends and keeping the Commandments won't be sufficient.

When Jesus speaks of self-denial, cross-carrying and life-losing, there's nothing in the Gospels to suggest that he doesn't really mean it. Peter made the mistake of supposing that the Lord was speaking figuratively.

"What profit does a man [or woman] show who gains the whole world and destroys himself [herself] in the process?" (Mark 8:36). That very question plagued Rose Lathrop during the years of socializing and self-aggrandizement that preceded her second conversion.

The first brought her into the Church, fed her on the sacraments, introduced her to the hero-saints. The second, during a concentrated retreat, opened her eyes to the waste of her own compassion, energy, talent and grace. She decided that the world held no profit of interest to her. Like the Twelve, she enjoyed the freedom of one binding decision to walk with Jesus. The only profit she sought was a place in his Kingdom.

In Matthew's account of Jesus' mission instructions to the apostles, a slightly different emphasis may help to bring the teaching home to us. Whoever refuses to shoulder his cross, Jesus says, "is not worthy of me" (Matthew 10:38). But what of those who do lose themselves in his love and service? Jesus juxtaposes ruin and reward, challenging the hearer to choose. "He who seeks only himself brings himself to ruin, whereas he who brings himself to nought for me discovers who he is" (Matthew 10:39).

Loss leads to discovery. Nothing is wasted in the Christian

economy—except that which is directed away from Christ. Disciples who bring themselves to nothing (in the eyes of Caesar's society) will turn themselves inside out and solve the riddle of identity. The person Jesus sees—through the latticework of psychological defenses, environmental influences and cultural accretions—will emerge into the daylight.

When he called each of the Twelve—Simon and Andrew from casting their nets, James and John from Zebedee's boat, Levi from his tax collector's post, Philip from Bethsaida and Nathaniel from under the fig tree in Cana—Jesus saw the selves that would emerge once these common men had cast themselves adrift from their everyday moorings. By losing all that they had been, they would gain all that they could be.

"What can a man offer in exchange for his life?" (Mark 8:38). The disciples discovered that to live with the Teacher under the shadow of the Tree was to be certain of the answer.

MEDITATION

We've been in Bethany for several days now, supported by the hospitality of Lazarus and his sisters. You might call this our extended sabbath: a time to rest and be with friends and taste the ripe fruit of leisure. "Come aside and rest awhile," Jesus will say. About once a month, or more often if we've been drained by the crowds, we leave the dust of the road behind us. Several homes are always open to us, and this is the one Jesus returns to most often. Martha and Mary, both beautiful, dark-eyed women of unexcelled virtue, worship him and make no secret of their affection. What man could be oblivious to that? Not our rabbi.

It would be impossible to say what these days mean to us. They are a breath of home. The sight of braided women weaving and baking bread. Sleeping deeply under the gnarled acacia in the courtyard, half drugged by its aroma. Time to hear the pensive song of the turtledove and watch the industrious house sparrows under the eaves. Talking quietly late into the night with the vigilant moon for our companion. Letting urgency slide off our shoulders. Being lulled by the music of feminine voices at dawn.

Without his ever saying so, we know Jesus intends these days as a time of threshing-over. He knows how long it takes most of us to get a firm grasp on all he's told us. And he expects us to work things out for ourselves as much as we can, sorting, applying, absorbing his words. Not that he would refuse to explain; it's just that we know better than to go to him before we've even husked and bitten into these questions on our own.

For myself, I'm turning over in memory that day at Caesarea Philippi when Jesus first predicted his death. Our hearts already felt like stones when he went on to assert that we too would have to take up our crosses and go to our deaths if we wanted any share in his glory. I remember the gooseflesh on my arms and the way my scalp prickled as he spoke. Fear had a stranglehold on my throat until I shook the images of violence from my brain. We were all horrified, both by Jesus' words and the determination behind them.

At first he spoke just to us. Then he began telling the local people about how the elders and chief priests and scribes would murder him. He even claimed he would rise from his grave three days later. Peter saw the looks people gave the Master. They obviously thought he was a madman or a prophet who had wandered in the wilderness so long that his brain had been baked by the sun. Several went off ridiculing the rabbi or wagging their heads at his sorry state. Taking all that in, Peter decided to set Jesus straight before he did himself any more damage.

I don't know what he said to Jesus. Maybe he blustered right into the topic like a camel on the loose. But whatever he said, it set Jesus off in a storm of anger. We had no trouble hearing what the rabbi said then. His black eyes shot stinging arrows at the whole lot of us. "Get out of my sight, you satan!" he commanded, accusing Peter of ignoring God's standards.

The poor fellow had the wind knocked out of him. He seemed to shrink by several inches. Jesus just turned and walked off. We'd never seen him like that. Andrew and John tried to console Peter while the rest of us sat staring like blind men.

Jesus had settled himself on a nearby slope thick with anemones and morning glories. Since he was so attuned to nature, we hoped those humble flowers of the field would have a gentling effect. After a while he called us and a group who had stayed on from the neighboring villages to come and join him. His face was calm again. Relief rolled the stones from our hearts. We thought he might tell one of his stories or explain his outburst. But he had something more urgent to say. And it was time for us to hear it.

"If a man wishes to come after me, he must deny his very self, take up his cross, and follow in my steps." Now every good Jew despises the cross. It is an infamous Roman gibbet for criminals and Zealots unfortunate enough to get the death penalty. The cross is an affront to our dignity, a barbaric instrument of torture, an emblem of our pagan rulers and their boundless cruelty.

How could Jesus ask us to picture him, whom we had just come to recognize as our Messiah, nailed to an accursed Roman cross like some no-account criminal with the rabble jeering at him and the soldiers defying his authority? God help us, we still yearn for a conquering Messiah, not a crucified one!

Not only must we accept his prophecy of suffering but we must look forward to our own participation in it. Does he mean these words literally? Are we to follow him into the chasm of death when, with a little moderation and care, we could live to a ripe age and accomplish many good works?

Silence helps us bear the weight of his teaching. That face we've all come to need as much as cool water assures us that Jesus does understand our sorrow and confusion. We do want to walk with him wherever he goes. He knows that. But painful as it must be to him, he has to show us the way.

"Whoever would preserve his life will lost it, but whoever loses his life for my sake and the gospel's will preserve it." This teaching penetrates more easily. We who have been by his side from the beginning have, in a sense, already lost our lives—at least the lives we thought would be ours, with the family and neighbors we grew up with, the familiar patterns cut by our ancestors, earning our bread in traditional ways, carving as much joy and comfort as we could for our portion.

Jesus watches us closely, an eagle determining whether her chicks can digest a bit more. "What profit does a man show who gains the whole world and destroys himself in the process?" he asks. This bone we're more willing to chew on. Matthew is smiling, having a certain expertise in matters of profit. He who had once measured gain in piles of hoarded silver and chests filled with embroidered festal garments, whose fingers had drooped under emeralds and onyx, whose table had attracted influential men and voluptuous women—he knew well what the Master was talking about. If Jesus had come just to save the tax collectors and the merchants, his question would be easy enough for the rest of us to evade.

Unfortunately, there are other and endless ways of destroying ourselves. For some, the appetites of the flesh croon a more seductive melody than all the world's riches. Others give themselves over to anger and judgment, envy and scandalmongering. For many, the taste of authority is addictive. How we love to influence others' views, see their faces uplifted to our wisdom! To be sought after for our opinions, to be flattered and fawned over like Herod himself is a powerful bribe—even for the virtuous.

I remember Jesus asking, "What can a man offer in exchange for his life?" He knew well that men and women seem all too willing to prize some things more highly than salvation itself. It isn't written out that clearly in their thoughts. But in their lives is the evidence. Their attitudes and actions suggest that security or influence or ease are worth the loss of abiding happiness. In more subtle ways good people are sometimes willing to subordinate God's will to family responsibilities, occupational demands or destructive friendships that separate them from Yahweh's flock.

I remember that Jesus sealed his discourse that day with a warning to whoever would be his companion. "If anyone in this faithless and corrupt age is ashamed of me and my doctrine," he said, "the Son of Man will be ashamed of him when he comes with the holy angels in his Father's glory."

No doubt Peter flinched at that, recalling his embarrassment at Jesus' public prediction of humiliation and rejection. Even Peter realized now that none of us could hide behind perplexity. Jesus' final word was that we had to accept wholeheartedly the prospect of creative suffering. Those who hadn't the courage and faith to say yes to that would meet with an averted face at the final door.

Several weeks have passed since that day. For a while we were all on edge, dreading confrontation with any elders who might report something scandalous about Jesus to the high priest. The Master himself seemed to feel much better. His preaching became more, not less, provocative. Certainly he had no wish to hasten death's arrival. But he did nothing to stave it off, either. We were nervous and fearful, but then something happened that gave us all a shred of glory to hang onto.

According to Peter, James and John, they had climbed Mt. Tabor with Jesus for a peaceful interlude. The three disciples were idly admiring the plain of Jezreel while the rabbi went on a little further to pray. John had turned around to make sure Jesus was still in sight when he saw him enveloped in a stunning light. Jesus' hair, his face, his tunic, his feet—everything shimmered in blinding white. All three disciples saw it and fell over on their knees, struck by the splendor of our beloved rabbi looking for all the world like the magnificent Messiah of our dreams.

Then—can you believe it?—Moses and Elijah appeared out of nowhere to converse with Jesus, one on either side of him. A cloud settled over them, as though they were at an exalted elevation, and the disciples heard a voice saying, "This is my Son, my beloved. Listen to him."* What a vision! What an

* Mark 9:7.

assurance, an affirmation of our fidelity to the Lord! Thanks be to God that we did not desert him at the crossroads.

As I lie here on my mat in the late afternoon stillness, I can see how it must have been on the mountain. I bear that image in my heart as a shield against the dark days ahead. If the cross is real, then more so is the glory. And we will share in it with him—the Messiah!

> May he live to be given the gold of Arabia,
>   and to be prayed for continually;
>   day by day shall they bless him.
>
> …May his name be blessed forever;
>   as long as the sun his name shall remain.
> In him shall all the tribes of the earth be blessed;
>   all the nations shall proclaim his happiness. *

(Pause for at least five or 10 minutes of reflection on the Christ-event you have just participated in.)

FIND A SOLITARY CORNER in Lazarus' courtyard in which to do your own threshing out. "What does it profit a person…?" is a many-layered question which Jesus expects you to apply quite differently from the person who strives after earthly gain.

Consider this question: What were some of the things you, as a teenager, hoped to gain out of life? Work your way up to your present stage of life, reviewing goals in terms of gains to be made in order to be happy or to be the kind of person you wanted to be. Ask yourself:

Have I considered a certain degree of success in my

* Psalm 72:15,17.

profession or vocation necessary to my happiness?

A certain amount of recognition from my family, colleagues, co-workers, community?

A certain amount in savings, insurance, investments?

A certain life-style to be achieved and maintained?

A certain reputation as a solid citizen, a reasonable person in religious matters, a member of the political, social or cultural majority in my community?

A certain degree of personal security to be preserved at varying costs?

Do any of my present gains require that I be less of a disciple than I know I could be? How or why?

Should one or more of these gains be let go of for the sake of Jesus and the gospel?

What difference might it make to my spiritual welfare?

If you are a person with sufficient income to provide for yourself (and your family, if you have one) a place to live, three daily meals and a modest wardrobe and still have enough left over to enjoy some entertainment or build up a savings account, what difference would it make if you regularly invested your gains in a particular missioner's work, a family suffering from unemployment, a peace or social justice organization, the education of a refugee or an orphan? Is this one way of losing yourself in order to discover another you might not have recognized until now? Remember, loss leads to discovery.

When you have finished your reflection, go into the house.

Sit down at the table across from Jesus. Tell him what gain(s) you will try to let go of in order to liberate the disciple within as he questions you personally: "What will it profit you to gain the whole world and destroy yourself in the process?"

CONCLUDING PRAYER

What are the swaddling clothes
    that wrap me round,
      binding the infant disciple?
I am oft held fast by tepid devotion
    that thrives on prudence,
      doing the reasonable thing.
My fiery dreams are damped by temerity
    that shrinks from judgment,
      conforming to the common way.
I am yet constrained by comfort and habit
    that recline with safety,
      avoiding the prophet's fate.

But when swathes are broken,
    Tabor's light flashes,
      confirming the Lord's formidable sway.

May I be free
    to lose all
    that's not gain
    to you.
    Amen.

CHAPTER SIX

WHO IS THE FAITHFUL, FARSIGHTED SERVANT?

> "Be sure of this: if the owner of the house knew when the thief was coming he would keep a watchful eye and not allow his house to be broken into. You must be prepared in the same way. The Son of Man is coming at the time you least expect. Who is the faithful, farsighted servant whom the master has put in charge of his household to dispense food at need? Happy that servant whom his master discovers at work on his return! I assure you, he will put him in charge of all his property."
>
> (Matthew 24:43-47)

ON THE FACE OF IT, Flannery O'Connor's discipline of writing two hours every day does not sound like much. Those who are not writers are prone to supposing there's nothing to it. Those who are would judge her time a minimum effort—unless they happened to know that O'Connor, probably the best of contemporary Catholic authors, suffered from lupus, a disease that devoured her energy and killed her in midlife.

She regarded those two hours with a sacramental awareness and would allow nothing to desecrate them. The books that emerged from her encounters with God at the typewriter were as finely crafted as early Shaker furniture or medieval Benedictine manuscripts.

Confined to the family farm at Milledgeville, Georgia, restricted by diet and medication and pain, Flannery O'Connor invested her talent in telling the stories of people possessed by the demons of contempt. Her contemplative vision of a world in which self-respect had fallen prey to hypocrisy, vanity and despair was far more religious than the pious unreality pushed by lesser writers. She regarded writing itself as a religious act. Even when she had to throw page after page of her work away, O'Connor did not count it a loss. Those seemingly fruitless days bore a direct relationship to those when the words flowed like honey. "The fact is," she wrote to a friend, "if you don't sit there every day, the day it would come well, you won't be sitting there."

Flannery O'Connor didn't talk about being a faithful and farsighted servant. She just was one. The Master had put her in charge of a small talent which, if vigilantly tended, would become a large and sure talent to reflect the world as God might see it. Although she had no idea when the Master might return, she was always ready. "Happy that servant whom [her] master discovers at work on his return!" (Matthew 24:46).

In the final spring of his earthly life, Jesus was possessed by a need to warn his disciples about the Endtime. He delivered in Jerusalem what scholars call "The Eschatological Sermon" (Matthew 24:1—25:46), stressing that the final judgment is always near and always a threat to the unfaithful. The disciples will be tested by political and natural disasters, tempted by false prophets and mendacious messiahs. "The man [or woman] who holds out to the end, however, is the one who will see salvation" (Matthew 24:13), he promised.

How would they recognize the Endtime? Let there be no mistake about it, Jesus responded. The Son of Man will rend the sky like lightning. The cosmos will be shaken as the majestic angels herald the Christ with trumpet flourishes. All peoples will mightily repent when they see him mounted on the clouds in glory. Then the chosen one will be plucked out of the multitude and gathered into one family to occupy the Kingdom.

Hearing all of this, the disciples wanted to be certain they were there with their auras shining. But Jesus couldn't give them the exact date or hour. Even he didn't know when the end would be. So he left it up to each disciple to make watchfulness his or her life-style. The man who concerns himself first with secular matters will be left plodding in the field when the Son arrives to whisk away the faithful disciple. The woman who is absorbed by this world's business will go on grinding meal, while her farsighted companion is taken.

To drive the point home, Jesus tells a trilogy of parables which echo John the Baptist's refrain, "Prepare the way of the Lord!" (see Matthew 3:3). He defines the good servant by contrast with the worthless one who resents the need to be watchful.

"If the master wants to take his sweet time about returning, I might as well make the most of his absence," the worthless one decides. Instead of caring for the other servants as he's been commissioned to do, he starves them and beats those who complain. Then he teams up with a troupe of drunkards and gluttons who occupy the master's property and consume his resources. One night, when the no-account servant is particularly self-confident, he beds down with a harlot whose panting drowns out the cries of the suffering servants. While he is thus appeasing his lust, the master appears in the doorway. The guilty one is soundly thrashed and thrown out into the darkness to grind his teeth in acrid anguish.

On the heels of that parable, Jesus narrates the plight of the foolhardy virgins who greet the bridegroom with their torches smoking and sputtering uselessly in the night. As they beat their fists against the barred door, the now unattainable groom insists, "I do not know you" (Matthew 25:12). Then there's the inept servant who, entrusted with a thousand silver pieces, buries the treasure out of fear. His temerity and stupidity earn him a tongue-lashing and final eviction from his master's house.

The true disciples in each story insure their eternal happiness by heeding the Son of Man's advice: "Stay awake…! You cannot know the day your Lord is coming" (Matthew 24:42). Flannery O'Connor counted her illness a blessing because it enabled her to see the wisdom of preparing for death every day. For the ablebodied and self-assured servant, there may be no more unlikely concept than the proximity of his or her end. Most of us find it more congenial to assign the advent of Sister Death to a suitable tomorrow.

When Jesus asked his friends to define the faithful servant, he didn't expect a simple answer. (If he had, there would have been no need of parables.) As his own death drew near, he would watch for the disciples' response in the witness of their lives.

MEDITATION

We can smell the sweet incense from here. The marble walls gleam proudly in the moonlight on the Temple Mount. Permanence resides in the massive ashlars of the outer wall which protect the esplanade. The noble girth and tiered chambers of the Temple itself, solid as the mountains of Ararat, promise that this house of worship will forever stand. Its columns and parapets point to the splendor of Yahweh, for whom this magnificent structure is no more than a humble tent.

We are country people who have stood each year at Passover in awe of the Temple's beauty, its power to proclaim Israel's preeminence among all the nations. When Jesus predicted this morning that the entire edifice would be demolished, we were astonished—even scandalized—that he would give credence to such a doleful prophecy. Sooner would we see the mountains tumble!

Now on the Mount of Olives overlooking the Holy City, Jesus is caught up in one of those moods that have infected him often in recent weeks. Words pour out of him, splashing against our ears in insistent waves. Peter has opened the floodgates by asking when the Temple would meet its ruin. (Personally, I think he was just humoring the rabbi.) Then Thomas interjects, "What will be the sign of your coming and the end of the world,

Master?" Jesus has been leaning against an olive tree, his face masked in shadow. But Thomas' question brings him bolt upright. "Be on guard! Let no one mislead you,"* he says sternly.

He begins to paint such alarming pictures of wars and disasters, torture and death, destruction and deception that we huddle closer together to defend ourselves against impending doom. "Because of the increase of evil, the love of most will grow cold,"† Jesus prophesies. His tone hasn't changed. Yet when he turns to look out over sleeping Jerusalem, immaculate in the moonlight, sorrow steals the firmness from around his mouth and he is silent.

The calamitous end will not come, he then continues, until the Good News has been proclaimed over the whole world. False messiahs will entice us with signs and wonders, but we will recognize our true Messiah by his sign illuminating the sky. The moon and the stars will forget their purpose. And a terrible legion of archangels, swooping on silver wings, will strike terror into the hearts of the faithless. Brandishing their trumpets, the angels will then round up the flock from the four corners, shepherding them into the presence of the Son of Man himself, resplendent upon the clouds with a gold-garmented retinue.

We are nearly dizzy from contemplating these unearthly images when Jesus replants our feet in the Palestinian soil by evoking the familiar fig tree. When the branches of the tree grow tender and the leaves begin to unfurl, lifting their broad faces to the sun, we know that summer is upon us. Just so, when we see the signs Jesus has described, we'll know it is the Endtime and he is standing at our door.

"But when will that be, Rabbi?" Thomas reiterates. He's a practical man, not given to dreams and visions. If he can't hold it in his hand or lift it from memory's storehouse, he can't accept it. Unfortunately, there's no consolation for the Twin this time. Jesus himself doesn't know the answer. Only our Father in heaven has it written in his book. And he guards it as jealously as

* Matthew 24:4. † Matthew 24:12.

69

he guards his Chosen People. So there's no sense racking our brains over it.

It will be as it was in the days of Noah. People went right on eating and drinking and marrying and singing as though they had no other purpose than pleasure. Even when they saw Noah and his sons working every day, fitting together the ark of survival, they laughed and paid no heed. "They were totally unconcerned until the flood came and destroyed them,"* Jesus observes flatly. He looks around, collecting our nodded assents. His glance stops at Andrew whose head is slumped on his chest.

"Stay awake, therefore!" The rabbi's voice impels Andrew to his feet with a half-witted lurch. "What? Who's coming?" he blurts, shaking his head like a bear startled out of hibernation. Laughter from the rest of us who have relished the rabbi's double meaning is his only response. Jesus joins in the laughter and waits for Andrew to collect his senses.

"Listen, friends: If the owner of the house knew when the thief was coming, he'd be on the alert to protect his property. Am I not right?" the Master asks. "So you must be prepared in the same way. Because the Son of Man is coming when you least expect him." Poor Thomas must be wrestling with that one. What would the least expected time be? When a man was in the middle of a grape harvest? When he was enjoying the delights of the marriage bed? When he was overpowering an opponent in a synagogue debate? Yet, if he already expected the possibility, it couldn't be the right answer. What a quandary for a down-to-earth fellow!

"Who is the faithful, farsighted servant whom the master has put in charge of his household to dispense food at need?" Jesus wants to know. Ah, now it's coming home to us. We've all been in charge of provisions at one time or another. A servant in that position would have to be trustworthy, reliable and smart enough both to divide and to multiply the available supplies— especially if the master's absence was of indeterminate length.

* Matthew 24:39.

The other servants would be dependent on him for their daily needs.

"Happy that servant whom his master discovers at work on his return! I assure you, he will be put in charge of all his property." There's not an unsmiling face among us. Having recognized ourselves as faithful servants, we can easily visualize our reward. To footloose pilgrims with no home to sleep in this night, the master's property looks suitably inviting. Several of us, in fact, would make fine administrators—if we hadn't forsaken such possibilities when we followed Jesus down the road to a destination only he could see.

Perhaps it's our self-satisfaction that prompts Jesus to proceed with his parable. What if the servant is a worthless wretch? A bit unsure of ourselves now, we decide not to plunge in with speculations which might wind up draped over our own shoulders. "But if...[he] tells himself, 'My master is a long time in coming,' and begins to beat his fellow servants, to eat and drink with drunkards," the rabbi continues; "that man's master will return when he is not ready and least expects him. He will punish him severely and settle with him as is done with hypocrites. There will be wailing then and grinding of teeth." *

The whine of the night wind emphasizes the chilling conclusion. Whenever the word *hypocrites* issues from Jesus' mouth, it seems to slither like an evil serpent that could kill a man with one bite. There's clearly nothing lower in the Lord's estimation. So if this worthless servant winds up in their company, his troubles are legion.

"Wrap up in your cloaks, my children. The wind is colder now," he advises, walking among us like a mother settling her babes for the night. Sometimes we're "brothers." Other times "friends." But when his need for a family is heavy upon him, we are his children. Even Bartholomew, the eldest, accepts it without grumbling, knowing that the rabbi's heart must ache for sons and daughters of his own flesh, offspring of his own spirit.

* Matthew 24:48-51.

71

"There's bread and a little goat's milk left over for anyone who's troubled by a growling stomach," Jesus adds. "Rest now. We'll talk more in the morning. I have other stories eager to be born."

He walks away from us, disappearing into the blackness of the grove. Wherever we are, however exhausted he might be, Jesus seeks his Father in solitude before putting his head down in sleep. He's never told us of this private prayer. But John has spied on him a few times. Not out of idle curiosity, of course—it's just that John loves the Master so much that he wants to emulate him as a devoted son would his father.

A few of the cloaked figures reclining on the ground are already producing a chorus of snores and wheezes. Most, however, are breathing lightly, thinking things over before giving way to slumber. Jesus always intends his parables to be chewed on and ruminated over. We've come to recognize them as the meat of his teaching and the source of our gathering strength.

Jesus wouldn't have told us about the worthless servant if he hadn't seen in us some evidence of heedlessness or preoccupation with the concerns of this world. As far as I know, he's never taught us anything merely to be passed on to others. His heralds are to live the message before proclaiming it.

What is this food, this property that Jesus will leave his servants in charge of when he departs? Ever since we've known him, he's given us only one thing: his teaching. By his words and acts, he has shown us how to live here and now so as to live forever with Our Father in heaven.

I'll never forget the first words I heard him speak. It was in Capernaum at the time of the Baptizer's arrest. Jesus looked the green young prophet then, I can tell you. He was already 30 but he appeared to be 10 years younger, as though the carpenter's trade had taken nothing out of him but built him into a sinewy David with cedar shavings in his beard and cheeks ruddied by his outdoor labors.

When he stood in the marketplace to address the few passersby who would listen, he was as eager and confident as

Elijah before the priests of Baal. Even the Baptizer himself couldn't sway people as forcefully as Jesus did that day. "Reform your lives!" he told us. "The kingdom of heaven is at hand."[*] Then, with his face burning like a Temple lamp, he went on to describe that promised haven where Yahweh would soon welcome his people. His words were so full of life that many of us would have followed him that very day had he invited us.

Since then he's taught us so much more, ladling out the truth as he saw we were ready for it. We are the light of the world, he said, charging us to stand up and shine regardless of the rejection that might be meted out to us. Turn the other cheek, he said, rather then destroy yourself with anger or vengeance. Avoid judging, or you will be sternly judged. Treat others with the respect you like to receive. Live the message, or the moths will consume it while you are procrastinating.

He must be reminding us of our responsibilities as disciples. When he is no longer here to prop us up, will we forget what he has entrusted to us? Will we despair of his return? Might we be tempted to count this all a dream when we cannot see the promise in his eyes? Will the Endtime fade from memory when he is not here to rouse us with hair-raising pictures of what will be? Could we ourselves become worthless servants, squandering his resources and starving those fellow servants who most need to hear the Good News? Who are the servants I would be most apt to neglect?

Despite our present faithfulness, we are all capable of falling away or turning back. Even now my heart shrinks from the prospect of the unknown testing that is to come. What if the Kingdom isn't as imminent as Jesus thinks it is? What if the years of his absence stretch before us like the wilderness of Zin, inhabited by poisonous serpents and devilish enemies? What if the persecution we have known as Jews is gentle next to that which we might suffer as followers of Jesus whom we claim as Messiah? These are dark questions I am not ready to explore.

[*] Matthew 4:17.

Heavenly Father, come to my aid! Jesus has urged us to call you "our Father in heaven" and to pray simply as he has taught us. But tonight I am threatened and the prayer of David, on which I have been raised, serves better to comfort me.

> I set the LORD ever before me;
>> with him at my right hand I shall not be disturbed.
> Therefore my heart is glad and my soul rejoices,
>> my body, too, abides in confidence;
> Because you will not abandon my soul to the nether
>> world,
>> nor will you suffer your faithful one to undergo
>> corruption.
> You will show me the path to life,
>> fullness of joys in your presence,
>> the delights at your right hand forever. *

(Pause for at least five or 10 minutes of reflection on the Christ-event you have just participated in.)

WHILE THE OTHER DISCIPLES are sleeping or meditating on their earthen beds, arouse yourself to consider the personal applications of the faithful servant parable. When Jesus returns from his night prayer, he will be refreshed and ready to hear your answer to his question.

If I had to define my household (as Jesus used the term in this parable), whom would I include in it?

What are the various relationships I share with members of my household? Which ones am I most concerned about?

* Psalm 16:8-11.

Which do I have least time and care for?

What might the food that my Master expects me to dispense be? (Recognize specific qualities, values, talents, truths that you have to share with others.)

Is there other food which I have been less likely to distribute? (Consider habits, attitudes and actions that would strengthen your witness as a disciple, but which you now find troublesome.)

Are there times when I am most apt to adopt the worthless servant's attitude: "I'm sick and tired of waiting for my Master's return. Today I'll do what pleases me. Tomorrow there will be time to plan his homecoming"?

Are there times when I starve my brother and sister servants by refusing to feed them though I'm aware of their hunger? Do I ever beat them with anger, intolerance, unjust criticism?

If I could know the hour of the Lord's coming, when would I wish it to be?

What am I doing to prepare for that day as though it were imminent? (A step in the right direction would be to plan your own funeral liturgy in detail. Another, to include missions or charitable organizations in your will, whether you are 22 or 82.)

If I had to identify one ministry to which Jesus has called me as his faithful, farsighted servant, what would it be?

The night is half spent. Jesus is emerging from the olive grove into the moon-sentried clearing. He beckons to you so as not to wake the others. Go and speak to him about what you have discovered in yourself, the answer to his question: "Who is the faithful, farsighted servant?"

CONCLUDING PRAYER

Oh, if you should come
      in the night of my anger,
      with the roaring lion aprowl within,
      then would I weep for forgetting.
Or, if you should come
      in the hour of my blindness,
      with the doors shut to the pleading poor,
      then would I wail for ignoring.

Yet, if you should come
      in the day of my watching,
      with the prayer lamp burning inside my eyes,
      then would I sing for remembering.
And, if you should come
      in the time of my giving,
      with the household cared for and wanting nought,
      then would I dance for faith-keeping.

CHAPTER SEVEN

*D*O YOU THINK *I HAVE COME TO BRING PEACE?*

> "I have come to light a fire on the earth. How I wish the blaze were ignited! I have a baptism to receive. What anguish I feel till it is over! Do you think I have come to establish peace on the earth? I assure you, the contrary is true; I have come for division." (Luke 12:49-51)

THE PARADOX of a peacemaker who causes conflict is at home in our dark age of nuclear weaponry and projected space warfare. The enormity of the threat forces Christians to take sides—or to be something less than their name implies. Avoiding dissension is no virtue if it is done at the cost of conscience. Those who refuse to enter the debate—or the fray, should it come to that—will do so at the risk of their faith. Both the Lord and the Church require us to shout yes to survival, and to explore every possible way to support that goal.

Since 1968 Daniel Berrigan, the Jesuit priest whose name prompts quick admiration or condemnation, has been disrupting things in the cause of world peace. Asked by the editors of *U.S. Catholic* why he persisted in his radical acts, he replied that the question seemed to him as basic as asking, "Why do you live?" or "Why do you breathe?" (July 3, 1980).

Many people are mystified by Berrigan's response. How could burning draft cards and spilling blood on the steps of the Pentagon be likened to such natural and necessary human acts? Most of us are caught up short when our moral ideals conflict with the imperatives which lie *outside* our skins—rules and laws, others' expectations, our fear of unpleasant consequences. We aren't accustomed to encountering people so driven by their deep *inner* convictions that they determinedly break laws they perceive as unjust and accept the consequences. We don't know quite what to make of them.

On the twin questions of nuclear arms and nuclear power, Daniel Berrigan says he has earned the right to break the law by trying to keep the law over a long period of time. He, his brother Phil and their community long attempted to involve government officials in a public dialogue. They came to civil disobedience as a last resort on a life-threatening issue.

By his active and open resistance, Berrigan has earned imprisonment and become the target of hatred and rejection from many in and out of the Church. But he has also focused public attention on the insanity of a nuclear mentality that embraces first-strike capabilities and speaks of surviving a limited nuclear confrontation. His witness has enabled others to act courageously in the same cause. He has helped them move out of inertia and beyond the "infinitely adjustable conscience" that can accept successively more immoral public policies. Daniel Berrigan has become a sign of division.

The disciples were probably stunned when the Teacher who advocated, "Blessed are the peacemakers..." (see Matthew 5:9), affronted them with, "Do you think I have come to establish peace on the earth? I assure you, the contrary is true; I have come for division" (Luke 12:51). What were they to make of such a declaration? Jesus had already shown himself, undeniably, to be a peacemaker. He practiced love of enemies and limitless forgiveness. Whenever possible, he avoided confrontation with the Romans and religious authorities. He had counseled his friends to keep peace in their hearts by avoiding any sinful example. Now he spoke of fire and division, of families divided against themselves because of him.

Luke's Gospel presents this provocative teaching in the context of a series of exhortations and warnings (12:1—13:9) directed either to the crowds or to the disciples. Jesus exhorts his followers to guard against hypocrisy and worldly fears. He insists that they recognize God's fatherly and solicitous care for them. And he reminds them that worthless servants will be flogged and tossed out among the untrustworthy. "When much has been given a man, much will be required of him" (Luke 12:48), he says, clinching the disciples' need to live in perpetual readiness for the parousia.

On the heels of the parable come three strange and disquieting images of a Jesus the disciples have yet to discover. He is a firestarter, an incendiary eyeing the whole earth and everyone on it. He is a candidate for baptism, not by water but by consuming flames. And he is a maker of dissension, a sign of contradiction—even within the familial household.

While the disciples are juggling these hot potatoes, Jesus turns to the crowd and lambastes them for ignoring the signs of the eschatalogical times. "Why ask me what is just?" he wants to know, implying that they are procrastinating and feigning ignorance of their moral responsibiities. If they don't learn to deal justly with one another, they may wind up rotting in an eternal prison, he adds for good measure.

Matthew's context for the division teaching is Jesus' mission instruction to the Twelve. "My mission is to spread, not peace, but division" (Matthew 10:34), he tells them. The person who casts his or her lot with Christ can expect to be set against those who should be closest. "Whoever loves father or mother, son or daughter, more than me is not worthy of me" (Matthew 10:37), the Lord insists.

Both Gospel accounts demand a recognition of the cross at the heart of human relationships. Following Jesus isn't all Sunday worship, righteous living and keeping peace in the family. By the cross, Jesus sorts the sheep from the goats, the radically good from the apparently good, the creative peacemakers from the apathetic preservers of an unexamined peace.

MEDITATION

The Plain of Gennesareth is crawling with pilgrims from Capernaum and Tiberias and Jerusalem. There must be thousands out here, as thick as dandelions. Some of our companions have set up a large booth for us near the shore where we can get out of the sun and grab some measure of privacy with the rabbi. Jesus must be assured by their numbers. Some come out of curiosity; others would follow a crowd off a cliff if they thought they'd find something worth gossiping about. But most, I'd venture, are genuinely seeking religious guidance. And who better could they turn to?

The rabbi joins us under a thatched canopy. Peter convinces him to quench his thirst with a juicy pomegranate that stains his fingers and runs down his beard. His enjoyment is as evident as that of a child who eats with no other thought than how delectable each mouthful is. "Want another, Master? We've got a dozen here for you to work on," James says, poking him in the ribs. "No, thank you, brother," Jesus answers. "They're too good to overeat." He reclines on one elbow, prepared to spend some time with us before returning to the multitude.

Earlier today he reminded us that the faithful person should never waste time worrying about food or clothing. That's the way of the unbelievers, he said, who refuse to rely on their Father's providence. "Do not live in fear, little flock. It has pleased your Father to give you the kingdom,"* he told us. No harp could have produced more appealing music. The way Jesus looked at us, we couldn't help but know how well Yahweh loves us—more than ravens, more than lilies, more than sacrificial lambs.

Now he seems constrained to repeat how vital it is that our belts be always fastened, our lamps burning. If we prove our faithfulness we will, in turn, be served by the Master himself. If we ignore our responsibilities, however, it will go hard on us— harder than on the criminals and prostitutes who don't know the

* Luke 12:32.

80

Lord as we do. Oh, we'll have a greater reward all right. But no one will hand it to us on a bronze platter. (Peter tried to finagle us out of our plight by asking Jesus if he intended the lesson for us or wasn't it for everyone? That got him nowhere.)

Jesus is sitting upright now, legs crossed, hands clenched on his knees. He's been quiet for several minutes, totally isolated from the chatter of the others. He no longer looks like the pomegranate-loving child. His mind is shadowed by some cloud no one else is aware of. Gradually, a mood of expectancy—or is it anxiety?—is communicated around the circle. Jesus gets to his knees, then falls back on his heels. Abruptly, he says, "I have come to light a fire on the earth. How I wish the blaze were ignited!" He seems not to see us, which is just as well. What fire is he referring to? Where is the bitterness in his voice coming from?

"I have a baptism to receive. What anguish I feel till it is over!" My God, my God, the Master is a mystery to us. The tears are spilling down the creases of his nose and over his lips. I'd do anything to stop the pain that's tormenting him but, in my stupidity, I cannot see its source. He might as well be speaking Greek to us for all the help we can be to him right now. But his tears give our concern no direction. We have to sit here and take it like dumb sheep at his side.

"Do you think I have come to establish peace on earth?" he asks, cutting us with his irony. "I assure you, the contrary is true; I have come for division." Oh, Lord, where is our peace-loving rabbi now? Where is our Teacher who demands love for all, even enemies? Suddenly the memory of him that day at Capernaum when his family stood outside in the courtyard unsettles me. Wasn't he a cause of division that day? No doubt his relatives went home arguing with one another and alienated from him. Yet he made no effort to restore the family's domestic harmony.

"From now on, a household of five will be divided three against two and two against three; father will be split against son and son against father, mother against daughter and daughter against mother, mother-in-law against daughter-in-law, and

81

daughter-in-law against mother-in-law."* He actually seems to take satisfaction in spelling out the extent of this dissension for us, as though he suspected we might be excluding certain sacred relationships from his prophecy. It's his way of telling us that no one is exempt from the rifts that faith in him must carve.

He lowers his head, waiting for Yahweh to take the world off his shoulders. We are with him in that wordless prayer that anguish will be banished, that the flames will not devour our rabbi with pitiless tongues. Perhaps Yahweh speaks to his feverish Son in the voice of the sea or the reassuring breeze off the water. Or perhaps he calls him in the voice of the people whose heads are waiting to be filled with Jesus' unorthodox wisdom. However his prayer is answered, the rabbi wipes his face, pushes his hair back from his temples and regards us with his characteristic composure. Then he goes out to feed the crowd.

Thomas, Judas and Bartholomew follow him in case he needs protection from the demonstrative listeners. The rest of us are left to grapple with enigmas. Fire, baptism, division—how do they fit together and what do they mean? We could sit here for a week trading speculations, but would we be any closer to the answers? Admitting that only Jesus himself can cast light on these prophetic statements, John offers to tell us what he thinks they might mean. Although we call him the Dreamer, we respect our youngest companion for his contemplative nature. He's a fair fisherman with the heart of a fine rabbi. So why not hear him out?

The fire, he says, might be faith in the Messiah, the Prince of Peace, who refuses to establish any earthly kingdom or to seek revenge on Zion's foes. Jesus would be eager to ignite faith in the heart of every Israelite—particularly in every Pharisee, chief priest, elder, lawyer and wealthy person who hasn't seen the truth of the Master's teaching. Would not such a fire purify all those it touched? Would it not blaze within every believer,

*Luke 12:52-53.

spreading from one to another, beyond the control of any who might stop it?

Might it be the irresistible fire of which Jeremiah of holy memory spoke:

> I say to myself, I will not mention him,
>> I will speak his name no more.
> But then it becomes like fire burning in my heart,
>> imprisoned in my bones;
> I grow weary holding it in,
>> I cannot endure it. *

John has us in the palm of his hand now. He loves the Word of God as well as any of us—probably better. "Go on, little brother. Don't stop there," James presses.

The baptism, unlike that which Jesus enjoyed in the sisterly Jordan, might be connected to the suffering and death which Jesus has predicted and we have refused to accept. What did John the Baptizer call him the day the two of them stood waist-deep in the river and heard Yahweh's voice? He called him the "Lamb of God/who takes away the sin of the world!"† If the fate of the Lamb is to be sacrificed, his death might be a second baptism in which all of us are saved, John reflects.

So as much as Jesus yearns to bring peace he must, John speculates, by his very nature as the Messiah, cause division. The Good News is only good to those who have ears to hear it. Others see it as a threat, an insult or a fantasy. All we have to do is recall the relatives and friends who have turned against us since we became disciples. They've decided we're maniacs or deluded visionaries and want nothing more to do with us. Jesus no doubt feels this more keenly than we do, but he must be who he is. And we must burn a little with him.

Thank God for John's insight. He's given us a pattern to look at, helped us make some sense of the Master's vision. Sadly,

* Jeremiah 20:9.   † John 1:29.

he's also raised the specter of Jesus' death—something that hits all nine of us at the same time. No one says anything. Nor do we waste any time leaving the booth to go and be with him.

(Pause for at least five or 10 minutes of reflection on the Christ-event you have just participated in.)

STAY WHERE YOU ARE. Feel the anguish of Jesus as he considers the kind of fate that awaits him in Jerusalem if he obeys the Father's will. If you cannot feel it, your intention and presence are equal substitutes.

"Do you think I have come to establish peace on the earth?" Jesus may expect a different response from his post-Resurrection disciples, who have the advantage of hindsight but the disadvantage of historical acclimation to the message.

Does a good Christian, in my view, avoid conflict whenever possible? Why or why not?

Does he or she avoid hurting other people's feelings when issues of morality or spirituality are at stake?

Does he or she obey the law in every instance?

Have I ever had occasion to put into practice the advice Peter gives in Acts 5:29, when he and the other apostles are on trial before the Sanhedrin: "Better for us to obey God than men!" (Acts 5:29)?

Can I conceive of any circumstances under which I might break a particular law?

If I had to name five contemporary people I consider to be outstanding Christians, would any of them be radicals, troublemakers, outlaws because of their faith?

Have there been times when my faith was a cause of division within my family or community?

Am I afraid to be baptized by the fire of rejection, suffering and death? Do I pray about this fear?

Have there been times when I've kept the peace at the expense of my conviction that Jesus expected me to do otherwise?

Are there current issues of grave importance on which I have kept quiet because I dislike conflict?

Have I spoken, written or acted publicly on moral issues such as the nuclear arms race, world hunger, civil rights, illegal aliens, abortion and capital punishment?

Would people who know me well consider me, in any way, a sign of contradiction to contemporary American society?

When Jesus returns to the shade of the booth, give him the cool water of your reflections and any resolution that has been engendered by his question: "Do you think I have come to bring peace?"

CONCLUDING PRAYER

Your tears assure me
That you too feared
And doubted,
Dreaded the flames.

Your bowed head tells me
Of hope that bitterness
And rejection
Could be delayed.

Your extended arms show me
That baptism by fire
Is ordained
For peacemakers.

CHAPTER EIGHT

BUT WILL THE SON OF MAN FIND FAITH?

"Once there was a judge in a certain city who respected neither God nor man. A widow in that city kept coming to him saying, 'Give me my rights against my opponent.' For a time he refused, but finally he thought, 'I care little for God or man, but this widow is wearing me out. I am going to settle in her favor or she will end by doing me violence.'" The Lord said, "Listen to what the corrupt judge has to say. Will not God then do justice to his chosen who call to him day and night? Will he delay long over them, do you suppose? I tell you, he will give them swift justice. But when the Son of Man comes, will he find any faith on the earth?" (Luke 18:2-8)

TO SURFACE-SCANNERS faith-keeping may seem to be a lost art. Sociologists say fewer Americans and Europeans are going to church. Journalists report conflict among Christians, Moslems and Jews in the Middle East. Philosophers verify the rise of secular humanism. If the Son of Man should come tomorrow, would he find any noticeable faith on the earth?

He would, no doubt, pass up the Gallup polls and the evening news, preferring to judge from direct evidence. In any Arab country, for instance, he could fasten his gaze on devoted Muslims permeating their mosques with zealous praise of Allah. And who knows? That might be enough.

In any country where Buddhism flourishes, he could fill his senses with fluttering prayer flags, chanting monks ("*om mani padme hum"*) and peasants spinning prayer wheels. And that might be enough.

In any Hindu country he could rub elbows with pilgrims in the millions keeping festivals, with yogis meditating and ascetics teaching toleration. And that might enough.

In a synagogue where Jews congregate he would be touched by true devotion to the Torah, the murmur of daily prayers and music of the sacred Hebrew tongue. And that might be enough.

In any place where Christians assemble, his ears would be gratified by the sound of brass bells, lusty hymns and Gospel preaching. And that might be enough.

But if he should stop at a cathedral in Moscow where, although the Mass has been outlawed for many years, Orthodox worshipers still kiss the icons and pray for the day of freedom, then his heart would beat faster. And that would be enough.

Even yet, should the Son of Man appear in Krakow or San Salvador and smell the incense of beleaguered Catholicism and hear the courageous songs of the people and taste the honeyed bread of their fidelity in persecution, then the heat of his smile would pierce the earth. And that would be more than enough.

Only Luke records Jesus' rhetorical attempt to gain assurance from his disciples that the faith would indeed be kept despite the trials that would soon begin. The question was appended to the parable of the Widow and the Judge, possibly as a warning to the early Church that perseverance in prayer must not be a victim of persecution. Whatever its historical origin, Jesus' question is true to its attributed source and crucial to contemporary Christians. As counterpoint to the insistent refrain, "Be vigilant! Keep your lamps burning," it speaks to us with affecting immediacy.

We don't have to be Pollyannas to interpret the parable and its commentary in an optimistic mood. The widow, by sheer tenacity and staying power, wins her suit. What she does, we can all do. Her success with an unjust judge is a pledge of our expectations from the kindest judge of all. If justice seems to be delayed, we are reminded that God is not bound by linear time and that the widow honed her faithfulness on the stone of the judge's obstinance. The final sureties are the Endtime and the Son of Man's coming to claim those who have not allowed his fire to go out.

Will he find faith on earth? The chorus of believers praising the Almighty and the Ultimate, whose manifestations are myriad and whose names are legion, will stagger the planet with yea-saying.

MEDITATION

Sometimes I wonder about Jesus. Always, to be accurate. He's so much like us—but so much more and more so. I'm not making much sense, I know. On a day that chatters so rashly of spring, who can bother about the finer points of rationality? Life has been so good to us lately that we've no time for apprehension. Jesus has been so often with us—not allowing his prayers and visions to carry him off into other realms—that the present has wrapped us in its fragrant arms like a tender lover. He's allowed us to come closer to him than we've ever been, and we're slightly drunk on this deep-running friendship that binds us.

His stories too are part of the binding. He's been weaving them left and right, up and down, snaring us with familiar characters and unexpected conclusions. Sometimes we snatch the moral right away; other times, it sneaks up on us after a few hours of our looking the wrong way. Whenever we're on the road, we retell his stories to each other so we won't forget the rabbi's emphases or the clinchers at the end. In the process, we polish up our skills as itinerant teachers. Then we pass them along at the next town to whet the locals' appetites. Once they've heard a good parable or two, they hunger for more.

Anyway, what I wanted to say about Jesus: For all his warnings and presentiments of suffering, he's been unbelievably happy over the past several days. Instead of talking quietly to one or two of us as we travel, he's been playing around, winning a pebble-toss with James and a wrestling match with Peter that wound up with both competitors rolling into the river. And he's been singing. Not just the Psalms, mind you. Oh, no. Folk songs about fishing and minding the sheep and finding a good wife. Sometimes he makes them up and we're supposed to answer him with some nonsensical refrain like "And the castanets clacked all day" or "The scribes they scribbled mightily."

At first we thought it was silly and only obliged to humor him. But he was enjoying himself so much, improvising lyrics and instigating three-part harmonies, that he dragged us along in his wake. What a picture we must make for the travelers who pass us on the road! Thirteen grown men, a few with greying beards, striding along and singing our lungs out like boys on their way to a village festival. Simplicity frees us from the harness of routine and acceptable behavior. God is good. And we know it. So why keep it a secret?

The Master is so full of life it would be impossible for him to do anything halfheartedly. There's such confidence in the way he carries himself that your own spine straightens when you see him. The playfulness that was hidden from us for a while has reappeared, catching us off balance and leaving us wondering, "Was he serious? Did he really mean that?" Humor has seasoned his stories and animated his narrations.

There was one about a wily manager whose wealthy employer demanded an accounting of his service. Having squandered the master's resources on gambling and loose women, the manager had to come up with a quick scheme or wind up digging ditches. So what did he do? The scoundrel sized up the situation with the cleverness of a hyena. He would ingratiate himself both to the master and the master's debtors by collecting less than what was owed but enough to appease the owner, who had given up hope of ever regaining his loans. Now Jesus didn't commend the manager's methods. But he let it be known that we ought to be at least that enterprising in pursuing our Father's business. Then holiness wouldn't be such a rare commodity.

His stories, you see, often make good use of the worldly folks who serve Mammon or self rather than the Lord. They, even in their blindness, have much to teach us. This morning, for instance, Jesus introduced us to the corrupt judge. The story went something like this:

In a certain city there lived a self-important judge who had no respect for God and even less for people. He took great pleasure in his civil position, wielding his judicial authority as a king his scepter. (Here Jesus mimed the magistrate's pomposity, a role so far from his nature that we roared at the hilarity of it.) His supplicants paid him well to settle their suits promptly. Those who paid him less well waited that much longer for justice to be dispensed from his well-oiled palm.

Now there was in the same city a poor widow named Miriam whose husband had died of old age and who had no sons to speak up for her. She supported herself by weaving mats for her neighbors until a callous nephew wanted to claim her loom in payment for a past debt. So she approached the judge, day after day, beseeching him, "Give me my rights against my opponent. If he takes my loom I shall surely die."

And day after day, the corrupt magistrate sent her away, seeing nothing he could gain from this indigent woman. He had not, however, heard the last of Miriam. Despite his refusal to decide her case, she returned without letup, week after week, to implore him. "Please sir, listen to me...." "If you'll just intercede in my behalf...." "Hear me, sir...." "I repeat, eminent sir...."

Finally, when she had beaten him into the ground with her entreaties, he said to himself, "If I don't settle in her favor, she will end up by doing me violence. I'll never have a day's peace with her around!" (The rabbi perfectly portrayed the judge's quandary. He made it clear that not even a heartless man could withstand the just suit of a determined widow. She persisted. He capitulated.)

The idea of a frail defenseless woman doing violence to a dishonest judge tickled us. We'd all known a few Miriams and crooked magistrates in our day, so the story in all its humorous turns rang true. If Jesus had said, "Look, brothers, you must be persistent in prayer and patient in awaiting the Lord's response," we would have understood. But how long would we have remembered? Now we had the inexhaustible widow to identify with. That is the difference between a savory stew and unsalted vegetables.

We knew, of course, that Jesus didn't intend to draw Yahweh as a recalcitrant judge. Just the opposite. What could provide a better contrast? If the likes of that character could be persuaded to do justice, how much more likely would God himself be to hear the pleas of his people? "Will he delay long over them, do you suppose?" the rabbi wanted to know. "I tell you he will give them swift justice."*

The Zealots among us perked up at that unexpected turn, as you can imagine. Jesus seemed to be promising that the Romans would get their due before too long. He sounded like David proclaiming:

> Rise, O LORD, confront them and cast them down;
> rescue me by your sword from the wicked,
> by your hand, O LORD, from mortal men....†

The King's prayer against persecutors echoes our hopes for a swift and sweeping justice.

Jesus watched us intently as we hammered out the meanings of his promise. The widow and the judge were temporarily pushed aside by the desire for vengeance which had animated Israelites for centuries. The new law of forgiveness for enemies and prayers for our persecutors was still a trembling shoot that would require long tending. We are infants when it comes to that love which is as noble and fragrant as an ancient cedar, as undiscriminating as sunlight, as beneficent as rain. No one understood that better than Jesus, a sprout of Jesse, a Jew like us.

*Luke 18:7, 8a.   †Psalm 17:13-14a.

"But when the Son of Man comes, will he find any faith on the earth?" His question brought us up short, waylaying sentences in midair. The rabbi's voice held no accusation, not even warning. There was a sadness to it and an implication of other hidden questions. I knew in my bones what he feared, how he needed to be reassured.

Underneath all his recent laughter and lighthearted camaraderie, the thought that he would have to leave us was an ache in his side. Would the Son of Man return, after whatever awful fate he so dreaded, only to find that he had been forgotten? Would there be no faithful Miriams petitioning the Father for the Son's return? Would the corrupt judges of this world with their polluted wells of justice be the only source of water his people would seek?

"Master, believe me, you will find faith," Peter said, pledging our fidelity whatever might come. "We will be well-watered gardens waiting for the harvester." Each of us affirmed it in word or embrace. And Jesus found relief in our certitude. For a few intimate moments, he was the child; we were the fathers grasping his hand to say, "All will be well. We'll be here when the time comes." It did our hearts good to know how much he relied on us. And there wasn't a one of us whose faith wasn't bolstered by this revelation.

(Pause for at least five or 10 minutes of reflection on the Christ-event you have just participated in.)

JESUS AND THE DISCIPLES walk on along the Jordan River toward Jericho. The valley is painted with crimson anemones, rose-pink cockle, golden narcissus and blue-petaled flax. It is spring, the season of anticipation and optimism. Slow your pace, allowing the group to go on ahead. Allow nature's confident renewal to enter into your consciousness. Consider the goodness of your own faith-keeping.

Have there been times when I importuned the Lord as persistently as the widow? What were the circumstances and what do they reveal about my motives and priorities in prayer?

If the answer to my prayer is not what I expected or if I do not discern an answer for a long period of time, how is my faith affected?

What are some of the reasons why God delays in answering (as we see it)?

How do I interpret "Ask and you shall receive" (Matthew 7:7)?

Of all the times of persistent prayer that I can recall, which do I now feel best about and why?

(Take a good look at the ways in which you have been faithful in prayer: prayer as direct communication; as presence and listening; as love of neighbor; as action in just causes; as fidelity in times of doubt and trouble; as forgiveness and mercy; as living wholeheartedly in the sight of God and growing in relationship with the Lord.)

In what ways have I encouraged and supported others in their faith-keeping?

The Son of Man is about to come to you with confident stride and expectant ear. Assure him that your lamp will burn even more brightly in the days that remain to you. And give him the answer your stock-taking has conceived in response to his question: "But will the Son of Man find faith?"

CONCLUDING PRAYER

Come, confident Lord,
in your splendor,
in your beauty,
reign!

"The Son of God, whose eyes blaze like fire and whose feet gleam like polished brass, has this to say: I know your deeds—your love and faith and service—as well as your patient endurance; I know also that your efforts of recent times are greater than ever."

(Revelation 2:18)

For love that endures wilderness fasts,
    may I persistently pray.
For faith that survives strenuous tests,
    may I tenaciously pray.
For service that fords rivers of doubt,
    may I unceasingly pray.

To see your fire,
hear your praise,
assure your heart,
is my intent.

Amen and amen.

CHAPTER NINE

D OES IT SHAKE YOUR FAITH?

After hearing his words, many of his disciples remarked, "This sort of talk is hard to endure! How can anyone take it seriously?" Jesus was fully aware that his disciples were murmuring in protest at what he had said. "Does it shake your faith?" he asked them. (John 6:60-61)

"IF WE LIVED in a State where virtue was profitable, common sense would make us good, and greed would make us saintly," Sir Thomas More observes in Robert Bolt's drama *A Man for All Seasons*. We'd have no need of heroes to prod us toward our better selves. Vice, however, commands such consistent profits that many find it difficult to practice anything more than a nominal morality. When confronted with questions of conscience, More concludes, people of faith "*must* stand fast a little—even at the risk of being heroes."

And stand fast he did, refusing to sanction Henry VIII's adulterous marriage to Anne Boleyn or to sign the trumped-up Act of Succession which denied the pope's authority to determine the legality of the King's marriage to Catherine of Aragon. He did so at the cost of his head. A man of stunning wit and surprising grace, Thomas More had everything to live for. But he would not pay the price of conscience for the privilege of extending his days.

To take an oath was, in More's view, to hold not only one's honor but one's entire self before God in a moment of truth. In Bolt's play his daughter advises him to go through the ritual of the oath, to say the words while affirming the truth in his heart. He can accept no such well-intended compromise. Desperate to deter him from prison and the chopping block, she tries to convince him that he's already done all that God could reasonably ask. More responds, "Well…finally…it isn't a matter of reason; finally it's a matter of love."

What more fitting witness could a Christian give? It isn't reasonable, after all, for Maryknoll missioners to risk their lives by aligning themselves with the poor and powerless in Central America, for Lech Walesa and the supporters of Solidarity to defy a well-armed government, for Catholic Workers to chose prison over payment of taxes to fuel the arms race. It's entirely unreasonable for Covenant House people to live in the Times Square sewer in order to redeem runaways, for Poor Clare Nuns to seek strict enclosure as a place in which to pray always for those who never pray at all.

Nor was it reasonable for the disciples to stick with Jesus after his synagogue instruction at Capernaum (John 6:25-59). His words could hardly have been more scandalous or revolting to those Jews who had asked for a sign of his divine authority. As John records the dialogue, Jesus is a visionary addressing a congregation of blockheads. The more he tries to explain himself, the more determined they become in their misunderstanding.

When he speaks of the bread of life, they hanker after a perpetual supply for their larders. When he says that he has come from the Father in heaven, they retaliate with, "You're not pulling the wool over our eyes, friend. We happen to know that you come from Joseph of Nazareth, a common fellow." When he explains that his flesh and blood are the source of eternal life, they fall back in disgust at the lurid suggestion of cannibalism.

Having explained all that he's going to, Jesus boldly reiterates the Eucharistic teaching without the slightest attempt to make it more palatable to his listeners.

> "Let me solemnly assure you,
> if you do not eat the flesh of the Son of Man
> and drink his blood,
> you have no life in you." (John 6:53)

There it is. Take it or leave it.

The response to his challenge is an uproar of quarreling, complaining and disillusioned comments as the crowd rapidly dwindles down to a committed few. The deserters include many who had followed Jesus for months, certain that he was the Messiah. This hard saying is too much for them. They turn their backs on Jesus, refusing to take him seriously any longer.

Jesus is unquestionably hurt by this massive rejection, both personally and as a religious leader. He could have avoided it by watering down the message or compromising with the disciples' literalness. But he would not. The time had come to ask, "Does it shake your faith?" (John 6:61). "Is the Messiah too much for you? Do you quail before the truth?" The line had to be drawn before the Master's theological demands became even more rigorous. If they couldn't handle this hurdle, they'd surely stumble over the next one.

What would those who couldn't say yes to the Eucharist make of Jesus' ascension to his Father? That image, he knew full well, would have them gnashing their teeth. "The words I spoke to you/are spirit and life" (John 6:63), he told them, recognizing how rare were those disciples who would discern the spirit of his teaching—and how much it would cost them to do so. They had cast their lot with one whom the common wisdom now knew to be a deranged prophet.

The loyal disciples stand fast. While they may be trembling from the force of the *ruah* whirling around Jesus, sifting the gold dust from the sand, their faith is not shaken. And they will, very shortly, have a chance to prove it.

MEDITATION

He was magnificent today. His words soared like golden eagles against the Galilean sky. The synagogue here in Capernaum was overflowing with people who had followed us from Tiberias, Magdala and Bethsaida. Many had been in the crowd yesterday when Jesus multiplied the loaves and fishes. Some were so taken by the miracle that they wanted to hoist him up on their shoulders and whisk him off to Jerusalem to be proclaimed king by common accord. (Their boisterous zeal allowed them to proceed without the slightest pause over how Herod and Pilate and Ananias might react to this plot.) Jesus promptly slipped away, hiding himself until darkness fell.

When we were ready to cross over from Tiberias to Capernaum, he had still not returned. Peter and James blamed each other for not going with him; John insisted that no man was better able to take care of himself than Jesus. The sea was already restless when we set out, and rowing a straight course was no easy matter. By the time we'd progressed 25 or 30 stadia, the wind had worked itself up to a near tantrum and Matthew was on his knees imploring Yahweh's mercy.

It was then that we saw the Lord. He was walking towards us with all the calm and composure of a high priest approaching the sanctuary. He called out to us: "It is I; Do not be afraid."* The wind's anger evaporated before him, making way for his peace. Yahweh was again parting the sea, saving his people from disaster. So many of us reached out for him at once that we nearly toppled the boat. We wanted to touch that splendid freedom of his that set him above nature's restrictions and humanity's poor imagination. I can't tell you how it happened. But just as Jesus came close enough to get into the boat—in that instant when we were focused on him—we were suddenly on the waterfront at Capernaum, safe and refreshed as though we'd just returned from an evening stroll. Nothing is impossible to this

*John 6:20.

Messiah of ours—absolutely nothing.

This morning we had breakfast on the beach, broiling fresh fish and breaking bread together in high spirits. What king could desire a richer setting? The blue sea shimmered before us. The low black hills shone like glass in the sun. All along the shore waves lapped at the anchored boats of our neighbors and relatives. Today the boats would have to wait while the fishermen came to the synagogue to hear the rabbi. Many of these people love Jesus as though he were a native son of Capernaum.

Once he began preaching, however, some of them began to wonder where the Master was leading them. A few who came over from Tiberias had the gall to demand a sign, as though the miracle of the loaves had been a trifle any rabbi could produce. They implied that Moses was a greater prophet than Jesus because he produced manna in the Sinai. There is only one bread from heaven, Jesus told them, and it is given by the Father for the life of the world. "Sir, give us this bread always," they asked him. And he replied, "I myself am the bread of life."*

That set off a wave of whispering and shuffling. But it was only the beginning. I wish I could remember all of Jesus' words as they came from his mouth. Never before had he been so eloquent or so confirmed in his own authority. Whoever believes in him as the one sent by the Father will be raised up to eternal life on the last day, he promised. Believers will never hunger or thirst because Jesus himself will feed them.

At first I thought he was so caught up in the glory of his message that he took no notice of the protest that was gathering strength among the skeptics. How could he claim to have come from heaven when they knew for a fact that he came from Nazareth, a town of no distinction whatsoever? A few graybeards who had known Joseph scoffed, "We knew his father—a simple carpenter. A good man, to be sure, but a son of the soil, not the heavens!"

*John 6:34, 35.

Jesus told them, "Stop your murmuring and listen to me." He went on, patiently explaining that the Father had sent the Son to draw all of us to him. The very words of Jesus came from the Father. Although our ancestors ate the manna in the desert, it did not give them lasting life. Only Jesus, the living bread, can do that. "The bread I will give/is my flesh for the life of the world,"* he proclaimed.

From every section of the synagogue, groups of disgruntled listeners left, shaking their heads and muttering against the rabbi. Did the sight of their backs convince Jesus to go easy? Did he then dip his words in a pleasing sauce to make them slide down more comfortably? Those who expected coddling were sorely disappointed. "Let me solemnly assure you," he said, raising his arms in a gesture of nobility, "if you do not eat the flesh of the Son of Man/and drink his blood,/you have no life in you."†

The literalists were horrified. Several stood, shaking their fists at Jesus before marching out of the synagogue. The undecided could no longer teeter at the chasm's edge; they too departed. Jesus had reduced the crowd to a few dozen disciples who were not yet scandalized. My heart raced as the impact of his courage and his intent reached me. How I wanted to soar with him!

None of us understood, of course. But we believed because Jesus had said it, and said it in such a way that to doubt him was to lose him. We gathered around him in the courtyard as the stragglers went off with loud complaints, intended to be overheard: "This sort of talk is unendurable!" "How can Jesus expect us to take him seriously?" "How stupid and gullible does he think we are?" Among those who walked away were several local fishermen and their wives, people who had been among the rabbi's strongest supporters. They were more hurt than angry, more disillusioned than offended.

Jesus watched them go. Then he sat down on the stone

*John 6:51. †John 6:53.

102

wall, his head bowed a little. Their rejection had knocked the breath out of him. The eagle had been grounded by his friends' refusal to fly. We sat at his feet and at his side—the Twelve, a few good men from Capernaum and Bethsaida, Mary of Magdala and several local women. The rabbi was silent, waiting for the pain of denial to subside.

"Does it shake your faith?" he asked. Oh, God, what a question! If it meant "Does it threaten the foundation of your religious assumptions?" some of us would have to say yes. If it implied an assault on our intellectual defenses of logic and reason, we'd have to say yes. If it involved a recognition that we did not know Jesus as well as we thought we had, again, yes. But we knew that none of these questions were in Jesus' eyes. What he wanted to know was, "Have I shaken your faith in me?" And to that, each one of us could say, "No, rabbi. We believe in you—now more than ever."

Peter roughly threw his arm around Jesus' shoulder, blushing as the women noted his affectionate nature. Mary rested her head on Jesus' lap and Ruth brought him a cup of water, letting her fingers linger against his hand for a second as he took the cup. No one said anything. Jesus drank slowly. Now and then he lightly touched Mary's hair. His gentleness still surprises us. The long years of wielding saws and awls, of hewing beams and planing frames, of chiseling and filing in his carpentry shop did nothing to rob his hands of their innate tenderness. (I remember once when I'd been working in the fields and sweat was dripping off me like rain from a lintel. His hands were still calloused then. But when he wiped my forehead and stroked my hair back, I felt like a boy being caressed by his mother.)

Then, as though there had been no interruption in his synagogue commentary, he asked us: "What, then, if you were to see the Son of Man/ascend to where he was before...?"* He was challenging us to walk on the water with him, glide with the eagles, hear the still voice of our God. If my flesh and blood do

*John 6:62.

103

not shake you, he inquired, what of my promised ascension to the Father? Can you accept even this? We stared at him, held motionless by the prospect of his manifest divinity.

Satisfied that he had winnowed out any remaining chaff, Jesus went on: "It is the spirit that gives life;/the flesh is useless." Ah, if only the literalists had passed the test and been with us to hear the conclusion! "The words I spoke to you/are spirit and life."* Yes, Lord, how well we know it. You and your words are one. You and spirit are one. You and life are one. We don't know how this can be. We can only hold on to it and pray for sight.

"Yet among you," he added, "there are some who do not believe."† What a chorus of denials that provoked! We looked around the circle, trying to detect any shade of doubt or hint of denial. Each face assured us the rabbi was mistaken. He had endured so much skepticism and disloyalty today that he had become overly sensitive, suspecting infidelity where there was none.

"Come, Master. We've all had enough for now. It's time to eat and rest. Come," Matthew invited him, beckoning everyone to follow. He had once owned a spacious and well-furnished home here, paid for out of the kickbacks he received from his Roman superiors. Since merchants from Philip's territory of Perea had to pay duties before entering the city (in Antipas' jurisdiction), Matthew had been in an ideal spot to line his own coffers—until he met Jesus. Then he gave it all away for the privilege of being a disciple. Fortunately for us, he gave the house to an aged aunt and uncle who were always eager to share its comforts with us.

Soon there will be wine and cheese, bread and lentil stew, fig cakes and almonds on the table. Jesus will pray the blessing and share our food. And, in a more profound way that we haven't yet grasped, he will be our food, the source of our strength, the flavor of our daily life, the gratification of our hunger.

*John 6:63, 64. †John 6:64.

(Pause for at least five or 10 minutes of reflection on the Christ-event you have just participated in.)

LINGER AT THE TABLE with Jesus and the other disciples, men and women enjoying the fellowship he creates among those who love him. Keep your eyes on Jesus and prepare your heart's response to his question, "Does it shake your faith?"

Call to mind the times when your faith has been shaken, either momentarily or for longer periods. What were the causes of your doubt: Rejection of religious teachings or practices? Rebellion against God? Separation from Jesus? How did you weather those times of testing? How did they reshape your faith?

At this point in your spiritual development, is there anyone or anything that might shake your faith in Jesus? (The death of a loved one? Loss of your vocation or profession? Rejection by an intimate friend or lover? Betrayal of the faith by a priest, religious or anyone you view as an outstanding Christian? Some new teaching or practice of the Church? A natural or man-made catastrophe of immense proportions?)

Is there anything in the Gospels that, if you were to take it very seriously and very personally, would shake your faith? Can you foresee any set of circumstances in which, like Thomas More, you might be willing to "stand fast a little…even at the risk of being a hero" for Jesus' sake?

When the meal is over, sit down with Jesus and tell him of your reflections. Remember that there is no shame in being shaken. He knows that from Gethsemane and the cross. The disciple who would stand fast must know his or her

vulnerabilities, must enlist the Lord as guardian and shade.
Answer his question honestly: "Does it shake your faith?"

CONCLUDING PRAYER

Would I tremble like an aspen before
     the winds of doubt or
     the threat of death?
Does my resolution quail before
     the rumors of war or
     the powers of greed?
Does my conscience falter before
     the suffering of the innocent or
     the scarcity of the saints?
Would my faith be shaken by
     intercommunion, women celebrants,
     lay preachers, empty seminaries,
     house churches, radical bishops,
     faith-healing priests?

Let me stand fast, Lord,
your word as my lamp
and my mooring.
For, in the end,
reason must waver
before love.

CHAPTER TEN

DO YOU WANT TO LEAVE ME, TOO?

> From this time on, many of his disciples broke away and
> would not remain in his company any longer. Jesus then
> said to the Twelve, "Do you want to leave me too?"
> Simon Peter answered him, "Lord, to whom shall we go?
> You have the words of eternal life. We have come to
> believe; we are convinced that you are God's holy one."
>
> (John 6:66-67)

CARLO CARRETO, AUTHOR and Little Brother of Jesus,
tells a story about a faithful stork. Although Carretto puts the
story to a different purpose (see *In Search of the Beyond*), it can be
seen as an image of fidelity. The Little Brothers, in an attempt to
protect the begrudging Saharan garden that fed them and their
neighbors, set traps for marauding rabbits, jackals and foxes. One
spring night, however, a lovely female stork, pausing on her
migratory path to the north, landed on a trap and bled to death.

In the morning, the rest of the flock took to the sky. But
the male partner of the dead stork couldn't tear himself away.
Day after day he circled the spot where she had died. His cries
and frantic searching aroused the Brothers' pity. They began
feeding him scraps of bread and meat, and he reciprocated by
attentively watching them, his elegant white head cocked in
concentration.

Every night he settled down to sleep in the sand where his
mate had shed her blood. For months on end, he had no fellow

stork for companion—only the Brothers with whom he could not communicate. Finally, the following spring, he joined a flight of storks passing over the desert on their way to the Mediterranean. His devoted watch was over.

In the end, it is not reason that matters, but love. We have no way of knowing what the immediate reaction of the Twelve was to Jesus' insistence at Capernaum that they eat his flesh and drink his blood; we only know they did not leave him. (The inspired author of John's Gospel, writing at the end of the first century in Alexandria, was more concerned about the response of the unbelieving Jews than of the true disciples. He wanted to show the Jews of his day, many of whom were attracted by Christianity but feared excommunication from the synagogues, the error of their ancestors' thinking.) We can assume, however, that the Twelve and the other women and men who remained loyal to Jesus must have been confounded by his totally unprecedented theology. The price they had to pay for their fidelity—in terms of intellectual assent, limited understanding, separation from more rational folk—was high.

The evangelist, after he has disposed of those who refuse to believe that Jesus is the Messiah, gives Peter, speaking for the faithful few, a chance to eclipse even the "beloved disciple." The aim of this Gospel is to persuade readers that "...Jesus is the Messiah, the Son of God, so that through this faith you may have life in his name" (John 20:31). So when Jesus asks the apostles "Do you want to leave me too?" Peter responds with the confession of faith John hopes to evince from Jews and Gentiles alike: "We have come to believe; we are convinced that you are God's holy one" (John 6:67, 69). (The credo parallels Peter's words at Caesarea Philippi; see Mark 8:29 and Matthew 16:16.)

The dialogue between Jesus and Peter foreshadows the final question-and-answer exchange in John 21:15-17. By that time the leader of the Twelve has fallen several times and suffered the intense shame of denying God's holy one. How much self-recrimination and regret he must have endured between the high priest's courtyard and the encounter with the risen Lord in the upper room! Peter wore his thorny crown of broken fidelity until that scarlet dawn on the beach at Tiberias when the risen Jesus made and served breakfast to his friends.

After that breakfast, Jesus offers his chosen shepherd an opportunity to be reconciled. And because love surpasses reason, the Lord doesn't say, "I hope you've learned something from your experience," or, "I forgive you for betraying me, friend." He sits down next to Peter on the pebbled beach in the morning sun, looks directly into his eyes and asks, "Simon, son of John, do you love me more than these?" (John 21:15). (It is a question we would give our eyeteeth, our worldly possessions and our hearts to hear. Not even the beloved John heard it addressed to him—only Peter, the first of the true believers.)

At first Peter doesn't recognize the nature of the test. At Capernaum, after presenting himself as the bread of life, Jesus was looking for reassurance in the face of the gathering storm: The disciples were leaving him, Judas' potential betrayal was already weighing him down and the envious were plotting to kill him. In this post-Resurrection encounter, though, it is Peter who must prepare himself for impending trials. The one who loves the Lord "more than these" must expect troubles and the cross. By his oath of love, Peter is bound to feed and tend as Jesus himself would do.

Even when he can no longer touch the risen Christ or see his face or hear his voice, the disciple is relied on to retain his or her fidelity. For just beneath the surface of the question "Do you want to leave me, too?" lies another: "Do you love me more than these?"

MEDITATION

The meal at Matthew's onetime home is over. We've come up on the roof to breathe the night air and let the stars remind us of our need for serenity. Our hearts have been strained to the breaking point with miracles and mystical pronouncements: the bread that could be endlessly divided until the last hungry mouth was fed; the water that unaccountably upheld Jesus and lifted us to the shore; the flesh and blood offered as food, the spirit-words, the ascension vision. How little of all this have we absorbed! Jesus has been speaking to us in the exalted language of heaven. But our ears are still made of clay.

Although some of us are less eager than others to venture further into these uncharted seas, it's too late to turn back. The truth won't come floating up to us while we wait, with dry feet, on the beach. Andrew plunges in. "Lord, what does it mean for the spirit to give life?" Jesus smiles at him, glad that someone has the courage to grapple publicly with these difficult sayings. "Brother, the words which I have given you and the life that I am giving you, day by day, and the life that I will lay down for you—these are the spirit-food which you must eat if you want to live forever."

The disciple's mouth is open in a concentrated effort to drink in this great draft of truth. "One day my spirit, which I share with you as my Father shares with me, will be set free from the flesh you see before you. And it will take up its abode in all of you who believe," the Master continues. If his indomitable spirit comes to inhabit us, then will we not be invincible too? Will we see with his eyes and speak with his voice and love with his heart? What a prospect that is for us who have to toil so hard at understanding and accomplishing our Father's will!

James's thoughts have turned to several friends who walked out on Jesus today. "What about those who don't believe, Rabbi? Will they return and receive this spirit?" he asks. Instead of responding directly, Jesus takes us all in with an encompassing glance. "This is why I have told you/that no one can come to me/unless it is granted him by my Father,"[*] he says. Does he mean that the Father has hidden the truth from those who deserted us? Or that they failed to petition the Father for

[*]John 6:65.

enlightenment, preferring their own lights to his?

John's attention has flown ahead to other disciples who were not present in the synagogue. What would happen when Jesus' latest teaching reached them? Would there be others who would depart our company and refuse to follow Jesus any further? Again, the rabbi gives no direct answer. He studies the night sky, and sadness creeps into his manner. We know by this that there will be others, many others. And every one will be a body blow to him. We too will feel these shafts of scorn and denial. The gulf is widening. We can no longer count on the multitudes singing Jesus' praises—or ours.

"Do you want to leave me, too?"

Jesus, that hurt. I wish you hadn't said it. No one deserves our loyalty more than you. And I swear there's not a person here before you who has—even momentarily—thought of leaving you. But if you pull back your tunic and expose the abyss of your need to us, we may not be able to bear it. Knowing our unworthiness to receive so terrible a love, some of us may falter or run away into the darkness.

With one accord, we look to Peter, pleading with him to close the wound that awes and frightens us. He is sitting back on his heels across from Jesus, and his expression tells us that he is in command of the situation. He leans toward the rabbi, lifts his shoulders and palms, orchestrating his own question. "Lord," he asks, "to whom should we go? You have the words of eternal life."

I'd love to whack Peter on the back or maybe baptize him with a barrel of vintage wine. If we had all sat here meditating for the next several weeks, not one of us could have come up with a better answer. To whom should we go? What perfection! But there's more. The unschooled fisherman is proving to be a silver-tongued orator.

"We have come to believe," he assures Jesus. "We are convinced that you are God's holy one." Convinced. Hear that, Rabbi? There are no waverers among us, no rocking boats, no scared jackals. We know without a doubt that you are the

111

Messiah. There is no other. To abandon you would be sheer stupidity and blindness. Do not accuse us of such infidelity, for we have come to believe.

The face of Jesus is a dark pool rippled by the night breeze. At first it reflects the consolation of Peter's avowal, the appreciation of one sensitive soul for the revelation of another. Then it changes over to a brooding complexion, as though the solace could not be sustained before an intruding omen. He has tasted the bitterness of myrrh and he can't forget it.

"Did I not choose the Twelve of you myself? Yet one of you is a devil,"† he says, refusing to look at any of us. The hopes Peter raised to high heaven quickly collapse. Jesus' wisdom has become a millstone. He is mired in doubts. Even the best we had to offer wasn't enough for him tonight. We are convinced about him. But he is not sure about us—at least one of us.

He had in anger called Peter "a satan" once.† He hadn't meant it for more than that moment's lightning flash. Now sadness or frustration over the loss of so many disciples disposes him to project impending betrayal and failure. We cannot take him seriously in this. Tomorrow he's going to see things more clearly.

"Lord, shall we go inside now for the night prayer?" Peter speaks quietly as he would to one who is ill. "Yes, friend. It is time," Jesus responds, standing and taking several expansive breaths. Perhaps he expels the thought of that unnamed devil, because his mouth turns up a little into the accustomed half-smile.

Descending the stairs with him, I am compelled to raise him again to the confidence and joy of the morning.

"Lord?"

"I'm here, brother."

"I will never leave you."

"I know."

"I love you too much for that."

*John 6:71.   †See Mark 8:33.

112

"And I you, brother. Forever."

*(Pause for at least five or 10 minutes of reflection on the
Christ-event you have just participated in.)*

BEFORE JOINING THE DISCIPLES for night prayer, assume
whatever position you find most conducive to meditation. Take
several long, slow breaths and expel each one thoroughly. Then
pray the name of Jesus for as long as it takes you to become
centered on him. He seeks the reassurance only you can give
him.

> Has there ever been a time when the responsibilities of
> being a Christian made me want to leave Jesus—for a little
> while or a little distance?

> How have I responded to others (particularly relatives or
> friends) who have left the Lord in anger or rebellion,
> skepticism or misunderstanding?

> In what ways have I been able to be a reassuring Peter to
> the needy Christ in others who face impending trials?

> If I had to name one way in which I have been "faithful as
> a stork" to Jesus, what would that one way be?

> Who are the people who have helped me come to believe,
> and how am I faithful to them?

> Before sharing my final response with Jesus, I call to mind
> all the reasons why—I pray—I will never leave him.

> Jesus is standing alone, just outside the entrance to

Matthew's house. The others are inside preparing for prayer. You cannot see him clearly, but you feel his presence and his expectation. If you can, tell him what he wants to hear in answer to his question: "Do you want to leave me, too?"

CONCLUDING PRAYER

In your imagination, join Jesus and the disciples for night prayer. Gather with several other people after sundown if possible, or better yet late at night. Create an atmosphere conducive to prayer by using large candles, an oil lamp or a lantern rather than overhead lighting. Burn incense, if you like, and provide music—either instrumental or recorded. You will need a Bible for the reading, as well as a volume of the Psalms (or individual Bibles) for each person.

Make yourselves comfortable on prayer mats or cushions, as Jesus and his disciples would have done in Matthew's house. As you alternate the recitation of the Psalms, hear in the leader's voice the accents of the troubled Lord as he prays with the disciples who could not leave him.

PSALMODY

Leader: The Psalms are bread in our wilderness, water in our Sinai. We have come together out of the darkness to pray in the light of Christ. Our prayer will blossom in this light and this silence.

(Allow five minutes or more of silence.)

Leader: How long, O LORD? Will you utterly forget me? How long will you hide your face from me?

…Give light to my eyes that I may not sleep in death

lest my enemy say, "I have overcome him";
Lest my foes rejoice at my downfall
though I trusted in your kindness.
Let my heart rejoice in your salvation;
let me sing of the LORD, "He has been good
to me." (Psalm 13:1-2, 5-6)

Companions: I bless the LORD who counsels me;
even in the night my heart exhorts me.
I set the LORD ever before me;
with him at my right hand I shall not be
disturbed.
Therefore, my heart is glad and my soul rejoices,
my body, too, abides in confidence....
(Psalm 16:7-9)

Leader: Hear, O LORD, a just suit;
attend to my outcry;
hearken to my prayer from lips without deceit.
From you let my judgment come;
your eyes behold what is right.
Though you test my heart, searching it in the
night,
though you try me with fire, you shall find no
malice in me.
My mouth has not transgressed after the manner
of man;
according to the words of your lips I have
kept the ways of your law. (Psalm 17:1-3)

Companions: The LORD answer you in time of distress;
the name of the God of Jacob defend you!
May he send you help from the sanctuary,
from Zion may he sustain you.
May he remember all your offerings,
and graciously accept your holocaust.

May he grant you what is in your heart
   and fulfill your every plan.
May we shout for joy at your victory
   and raise the standards in the name of our
     God.
   The LORD grant you all your requests!

               (Psalm 20:1-6)

(Allow several minutes of silence.)

Leader: O LORD, I love the house in which you dwell,
     the tenting-place of your glory. (Psalm 26:8)

Companions: One thing I ask of the LORD,
     this I seek:
  To dwell in the house of the LORD
     all the days of my life.... (Psalm 27:4)

Leader: Love the LORD, all you his faithful ones!
     The LORD keeps those who are constant,
     but more than requites those who act proudly.
  Take courage and be stouthearted,
     all you who hope in the LORD.

              (Psalm 31:24-25)

Companions: For this shall every faithful person pray to you
     in time of stress.
  Though deep waters overflow,
     they shall not reach him.
  You are my shelter; from distress you will
       preserve me;
     with glad cries of freedom you will ring me
       round. (Psalm 32:6-7)

Leader: I will instruct you and show you the way
     you should walk;

I will counsel you, keeping my eye on you.
(Psalm 32:8)

(Allow several minutes of silence.)

READING

Romans 8:35-39, Indomitable Love for Christ.

(Pause for silent reflection.)

RESPONSE

Music or spontaneous petitions.

COLLECT

All: Lord Jesus,
you ask if we would leave you.
Remembering the days of our forgetting,
of our rebelling,
of our uncaring,
of our neglecting,
we know the answer cannot be rooted in our own
strength.
Our impoverished soil will not sustain the faith you
seek.
You must be the answer, as well as the question.

Lord Jesus,
we will never leave you.
Not as long as your Word is spoken,
Not as long as your bread is broken,
Not as long as your nets are mended,
Not as long as your vines are tended.
For as long as your lamp shatters our dark,
For as long as your Spirit impels our heart,

Lord Jesus,
we will never leave you.

So be it forever and ever, amen.